# HIGHGATE PAST

# HIGHGATE PAST

## A Visual History of Highgate

by
John Richardson

HISTORICAL PUBLICATIONS

First published 1989
by Historical Publications Ltd.
54 Station Road, New Barnet, Herts
and 32 Ellington Street, N7
(Telephone 01–607 1628)

ISBN 0 948667 02 8

Typeset by Historical Publications Ltd.
and Fakenham Photosetting Ltd.
Printed in Great Britain by
Biddles Ltd, Guildford and King's Lynn

# Contents

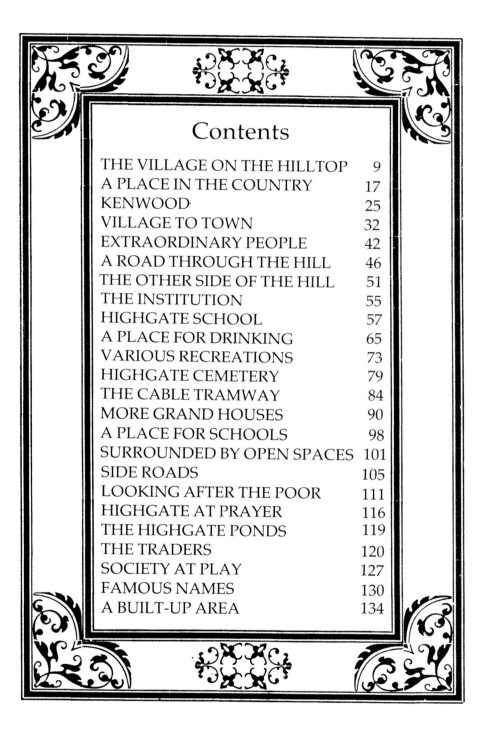

# The Illustrations

The following have kindly allowed the publication of illustrations:

*Peter Barber*, 37.
*British Library*, 34.
*M.J. Hammerson*, 95, 100, 117, 130, 135, 172.
*The Highgate Literary and Scientific Institution*, 45, 48, 53, 54, 91, 92, 96, 97, 115, 125, 129, 136, 139, 144, 151, 152, 153, 154.
*Highgate School*, 56, 57, 58, 60, 61, 62, 63, 64, 65.
*London Borough of Camden*, 77, 78, 84, 85, 88, 89, 101, 105, 106, 110, 113, 122, 126, 133, 134, 140, 150, 156, 171.
Other illustrations are from the collection of Historical Publications Ltd.

The cover illustration (which is also printed in the text) is of Kentish Town House (1787), and is reproduced by kind permission of the British Library.

# Introduction

Despite the close proximity of central London Highgate remains recognisably a large village – at least in London terms. Its pace and atmosphere have changed most in the last ten or so years. Increased traffic, spiralling house prices, and a gradual tendency for the shops to cater for visitors and house buyers, have made the place more frenetic and less relaxing. But a village which was made prosperous in the past from its London trade can hardly complain that its association with the capital now weighs too heavily. What it has to do is be vigilant in keeping the features that are so admired.

The past has left a substantial visual history and it has been a pleasure selecting what I hope is a representative range of illustrations to record Highgate's history. Some pictures are well-known, but it would be perverse to omit them. Others are new or rarely printed. If they only bring a warm feeling of nostalgia they would justify their reproduction, but when looked at without haste and in detail they reveal a great deal about Highgate and its buildings.

In the assembly of the pictures I have received much help from Gwynydd Gosling, librarian of the Highgate Literary and Scientific Institution, and Malcolm Holmes and Richard Knight of the Local History Library of the London Borough of Camden. I am also much indebted to Peter Barber for many kindnesses and suggestions. I am grateful also to Theodore Mallinson of Highgate School, and to M.J. Hammerson for allowing me to choose pictures freely from their collections.

John Richardson

# Further Reading

Useful books on the Highgate area are as follows:
Survey of London Vol. 17, *The Village of Highgate*, (1936).
Victoria County History, *Middlesex, Vol. 1*, (1969).
Victoria County History, *Middlesex, Vol. 6*, (1980).
*The Early Records of Harringay alias Hornsey*, by S.J. Madge (1938).
*The Mediaeval Records of Harringay alias Hornsey*, by S.J. Madge (1939).
*Court Rolls of the Bishop of London's Manor of Hornsey 1603–1701*, by William McBeath Marcham and Frank Marcham, (1929).
*The History and Antiquities of Highgate*, by Frederick Prickett, (1842).
*The History, Topography and Antiquities of Highgate*, by John H. Lloyd, (1888).
*Old Highgate*, by Sydney Kitchener.
*Highgate: Its History since the Fifteenth Century*, by John Richardson, (1983).

There are, as well, numerous smaller books and pamphlets on specialised local subjects. Many of these are listed in the bibliography of *Highgate: Its History since the Fifteenth Century* by John Richardson. Otherwise the local collections of the Highgate Literary and Scientific Institution, and the London Boroughs of Camden, Haringey and Islington, should be consulted.
Talks are frequently given on Highgate related subjects at meetings of the Camden History Society, Swiss Cottage Library, Avenue Road, NW3 and the Hornsey Historical Society, The Old Schoolhouse, 136 Tottenham Lane, N8, whose publications include articles on the area.

1. *View from the Slopes of Highgate Archway*, a drawing by T.M. Baynes published in 1822. This view looks south towards the City of London. It gives an idea of the sort of hill encountered by travellers through Highgate before the Archway Road, shown in the foreground, was constructed.

# The Village on the Hilltop

## A FORMIDABLE HILL

Hills are mixed blessings. In Highgate, even the poorest residents of the 15th century would have had superb views from their gardens (for it is unlikely they had windows in their houses). East, west and north, but especially south, where the distinct shapes of the cities of London and Westminster sat on the Thames, the views must have compensated for much. The gothic spires of pre-Fire London were visible and their bells audible – the legend of Dick Whittington listening to Bow Bells while on the slopes of Highgate has, at least, *that* element of accuracy if no other.

Not so enamoured of the hill were travellers. The main road north from the City was the York Way-Brecknock Road-Dartmouth Park Hill route. At Highgate they could either go across the ridge which carried the lane to Hornsey or else go further up the village and at the Gatehouse use the toll road (to-day's North Road) that the Bishop of London had cut across his land in the late 13th century. The climb for man and beast was arduous at the best and in the winter could be impossible. Thousands of animals on their way to slaughter at Smithfield were herded down the High Street and their hooves wore away the primitive surface of the road so that one bout of rain could reduce it to thick mud. That some of the animals went astray in the village is shown in a manor court record of 1485 when a London butcher was fined for illegally retrieving 8 oxen and bullocks from the Highgate pound without payment.

The profusion of pubs in the village underlines Highgate's long-term role – to refresh the traveller before the descent or to revive him after the climb. The oldest inn probably stood on the site of the Angel, but the Gatehouse next to the tollhouse leaves no record until the 17th century. By 1552 there were five inns in the village and, no doubt, a number of alehouses as well. Pubs, after all, sold many of the necessities of life. Apart from the ale which people of all ages drank instead of water, inns retailed food and vegetables.

## ON THE FRINGE OF THINGS

Highgate then, as now, was divided over three authorities. North of the High Street was Hornsey, south was St Pancras and, south east of Hornsey Lane, Islington held sway – three boundaries met, as now, by Lauderdale House. Complicating this multi-parish control were the four manors in the area, still, until the late 17th century, responsible for road maintenance, registering property title, the punishment of minor misdemeanours, the scouring of ditches and the mending of fences.

More important than the conjunction of the parishes was the fact that Highgate was far from the centre of any of them. The administration of Hornsey was then still in that village, that for St Pancras had shifted to Kentish Town, and Islington was little more than a settlement around Islington Green. Part of three parishes the village may have been, but its isolation helped to develop an entity for Highgate, though still without self-governance. Also, the three parish churches to which the residents of Highgate had allegiance and duty were a long journey away, especially on inhospitable days. This geographical difficulty led to the establishment of Highgate Chapel.

2. *View looking down Highgate Hill*, by T.M. Baynes, 1822. This, one of the best-known Highgate views, shows The Bank on the left with Cromwell House visible and Winchester House beyond it. On the right are the gates of Lauderdale House and the old Black Dog pub on the site of St Joseph's.

*3. Highgate Old Chapel.* **This building was erected on the site of the old hermitage** *c*1578 **and mostly taken down in 1833. It
served not only the pupils of the school but the population of Highgate as well.**

A hermitage existed in the village by 1364 – its occupant divided his time between contemplation, managing the toll gate and resurfacing the main road. When the chapel was established, or developed from this hermitage, is not clear but it was here, dedicated to St Michael, the protector of places on high ground, before Highgate School and its own chapel were founded. No doubt some answers lie beneath the old graveyard.

In effect, Highgate Chapel functioned as a 'chapel-of-ease'. This quaint phrase denoted a church to which parishioners were permitted to go more easily for much of the year, rather than to the distant parish church, provided that the income from collections and other services still went to the vicar of the parish. The trouble at Highgate was that the school chapel owed no allegiance to any of the parish churches and the vicars of Hornsey, St Pancras and Islington were the poorer. Friction was inevitable and even before the school chapel was built, the poor hermit was 'visited' by the vicar of St Pancras and at least forty supporters in 1503; the hermit felt sufficiently menaced to hide in the steeple and later to take his case to the Star Chamber.

*4. View of Highgate in Middlesex taken from Upper Holloway.* A mid–18th century view that seems to underestimate the hill up to Highgate, but it does emphasise the nature of the road surface.

5. *Dorchester House.* This building can be traced back to the 16th century, when it was called 'The Blewhouse'; the 1st Marquess of Dorchester owned it in the 17th century. It was demolished *c*1688 and its gardens taken up by the new houses of The Grove.

The settlement in Highgate of quite wealthy people began in the 16th century. We know of at least six large houses in the village before James I came to the throne. One was a 'capital messuage' on the site of Fairseat in the High Street, the supposed residence of Sir Roger Cholmeley, founder of Highgate School. A second was what became Dorchester House; this stood between today's Witanhurst and The Grove, together with 32 acres to its rear. A third was on the site of Lauderdale House, and a fourth, what became Arundel House, on the site of The Old Hall. Nearby, a mansion stood between Swains Lane and the site of the old Congregational Church in South Grove; this was here by 1580. Almost certainly at least one mansion stood on the Hornsey side of Highgate Hill, on roughly the site of Channing School. It may be concluded from the fact of this relatively large number of mansions in so small a village that local people would have had employment in plenty, either working on the estates and in the houses or else supplying them with goods. Otherwise the main village clustered around Pond Square, which was then a green containing-two ponds. To its west, on the site of the reservoir by The Grove, a third pond existed.

At an early date, therefore, Highgate had taken on a character not dissimilar to the one it has today, of small houses clinging to the brow of the hill surrounded by quite substantial mansions owned or occupied by people who were essentially creatures of the capital. It was a trend to be underlined in the next century.

THE OLD GATEWAY
HIGHGATE HILL
DEMOLISHED 1769.

6. *The Old Gateway, Highgate Hill.* The Bishop of London built a toll road, now North Road and North Hill, through his estate in the 14th century. No doubt the Gatehouse tavern developed from the acumen of successive toll keepers, for eventually the entrance to the road, the collector's hut and the tavern were an integrated group of buildings.

*7. The Old Gate House and Chapel*, by D.W. Wolstenholme. A mid–18th century print which shows, probably, the first Gatehouse tavern. Note also differences in the Chapel compared with *Illustration 3*: the tower has no steeple and the side roof has gables.

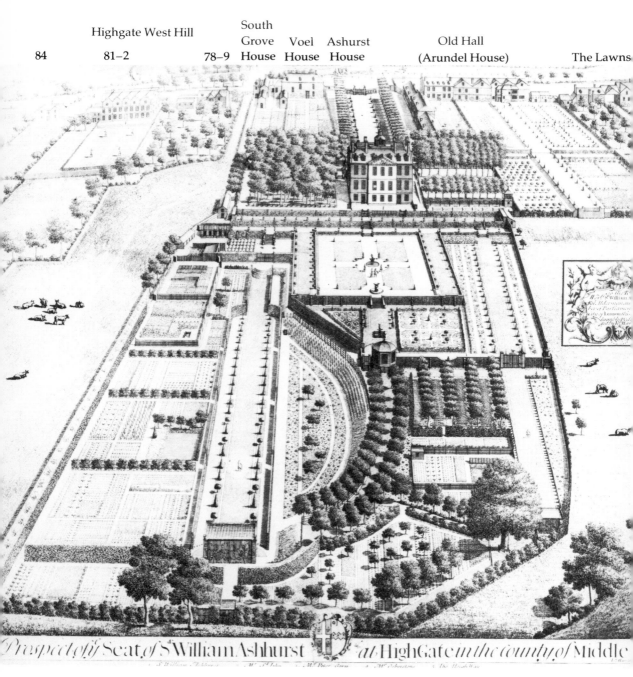

Highgate West Hill    South Grove House    Voel House    Ashurst House    Old Hall (Arundel House)    The Lawns

84    81–2    78–9

*8. A Prospect of the Seat of Sir William Ashurst at Highgate, c1710, from an engraving by W. Harris. Ashurst House itself occupies the site of today's St Michael's church and the grounds were later absorbed into the older Highgate Cemetery. Bromwich Walk, an ancient footpath leading from Swains Lane, emerges to the left of South Grove House.*

# A Place in the Country

## LONDON EXPANDS

Around London in the 17th century the tiny villages expanded. Fulham, Chelsea, Hackney, Hampstead and Highgate, among others, were sought out by aristocrats, gentry and merchants. As the activities of court, commerce and law stabilised and grew in the capital, despite the disorganisation of the Civil War period, so there was a demand for houses outside the crowded City. The Great Fire of 1666 made them even more necessary.

Some influential people came to Highgate, a place with much to recommend it. Within convenient distance of London, it was rural, tranquil and, like Hampstead along the same ridge, it had good air and views. More specifically, Highgate had religious advantages. Parliament in 1665 inhibited non-conformist ministers from preaching within five miles of London, and Highgate, just beyond that limit, attracted both preachers and their congregations who, quite frequently, were from the wealthy merchant class.

From this period Highgate derived much prosperity and some of its better known houses. Arundel House, now The Old Hall, brought fame to Highgate. Strictly speaking, as *Illustration 8* shows, the original house was 16th century, and John Norden, writing in 1593 described its attractions and views over London, the Thames and Greenwich. In 1610 the 2nd Earl of Arundel bought the house. He was one of the most celebrated art collectors and patrons of the century, and is said to have brought the artist Wenceslaus Hollar to London, and to have discovered the talent of Inigo Jones. One friend was Francis Bacon who, having caught a chill in Swains Lane while attempting an early experiment in preserving meat in snow, died at Arundel House in 1626.

The most prominently displayed house in *Illustration 8* is Ashurst House, occupied by Sir William Ashurst, Lord Mayor of London. His mansion was either an early 18th century rebuilding, or an adaptation, of a 'Banqueting House', possibly built by Arundel himself, and its former name implies a substantial and consistent amount of entertaining in the village at the time. This estate plan, portraying gar-

9. *Old Hall, South Grove.* A drawing by W. West at the beginning of this century. The original house, depicted in *Illustration 8* was bought by the 2nd Earl of Arundel in 1610 – it was here that Francis Bacon died.

dens that ran over much of the area of today's old Highgate Cemetery, shows the Ashurst property to its best advantage and its contours may be traced right down to the present day.

Opposite was a large house on the site of today's Witanhurst. Called Parkfield for much of its existence, it can be traced to 1665 when a London apothecary sold it to a London draper.

Mention has already been made of Dorchester House opposite. In the reign of Charles I the Marquess of Dorchester had taken up residence here; he managed to hold on to his estates despite his early opposition to Parliament during the Civil War period. His house did not long survive him however. It was demolished by the end of the 17th century and in its garden The Grove was built, or at least the first six houses that we see today on the crest of the hill.

These houses were part of the bizarre plan in the 1680s of a gentleman called William Blake, to form a school for London orphans (called a 'Ladyes Hospitall'). He bought not only the Banqueting House but also Dorchester House, together with land on the site of The Flask. An aerial view of his plan is shown in *Illustration 10*, much out of scale, but it is unclear if the school was opened, or even where it was. The purchase of all these properties to bring about such a modest purpose bankrupted him and he was obliged to sell them and abandon his scheme

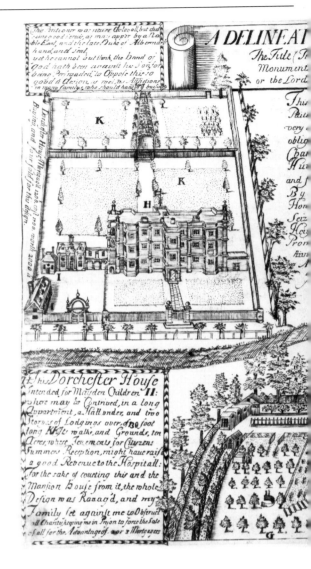

10. *A Delineation of the Ladyes Hospital at Highgate.* A plan drawn up by William Blake in c1688. Blake's scheme was for a home and school (hospital) for poor children from London, based on the subscriptions of ladies of affluence. His venture was not favoured by his family and it eventually drove him into bankruptcy. 'Highgate Road' marks the route of Highgate West Hill on its way to the Gatehouse. 'H', top left, is Dorchester House, a representation which compares quite closely with *Illustration 5*. What is now South Grove is not shown but it most certainly ran between the two principal buildings in the foreground. On the left (E) is the original Banqueting House, built as an attachment to the Old Hall, which is not shown. The school itself is depicted on the right, on the site of The Flask and its hinterland. It is not clear if the school was ever built.

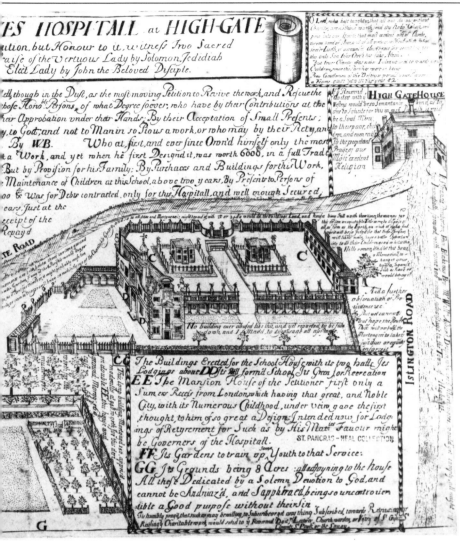

Lauderdale House derived its name in the 17th century from its ownership by the unpopular Earl of Lauderdale, who was described as 'a bold and unabashed liar' and 'the most dishonest man in the whole cabal'. But the original house, traces of which remain in the present structure, was probably built at the end of the 16th century when Richard Martin, a goldsmith, was living here. Two traditions are connected with Lauderdale House. One is that Nell Gwyn stayed here (and so, presumably, did Charles II), and the other is that she threatened to drop their son out of a top floor window if the king did not bestow a title on him. The babe became the Duke of St Albans, and, oddly enough, a 19th-century descendant occupied the Holly Lodge estate next door. Like other large Highgate houses from the 18th century onwards, Lauderdale House made an ideal place for a private school or convalescent home of some kind. It was given by Sir Sydney Waterlow to the London County Council in 1889.

On the other side of Highgate Hill, on the rise of land called The Bank, Cromwell House was built about 1638 by Sir Richard Sprignell; it is regarded as one of the best examples of houses of the period. The name of the house is a mystery, for there appears to have been no connection between the house and Cromwell or his son-in-law Henry Ireton, except that when Sprignell died a lunatic in 1659, one of the trustees of his will was John Ireton who lived in Lauderdale House: he was the brother of Cromwell's famous general. In recent years the future of Cromwell House has looked bleak. Left empty it has suffered much vandalism and damage, particularly to the carved staircase, and it was the subject of a number of conversion plans, all defeated by local conservation groups and Haringey Council. It has recently been restored to a high standard.

Further towards the village on the same Bank was a house owned during the Commonwealth by Sir John Wollaston, a London goldsmith, who also bought the manor of Hornsey once the king had been deposed. *Illustration 14* shows it to have what appears to be an Elizabethan wing.

Wollaston's name is also connected with the almshouses in Southwood Lane. His bequest led to the building of six dwellings in 1669 and these were

11. *Lauderdale House*, by W. West, *c*1905.

12. *A scene on The Bank, Highgate Hill.*

13. *Cromwell House*, by A.R. Quinton, published in *The Annals of Hampstead* by Barratt (1912). At the time of the drawing it was occupied by the Hospital for Sick Children.

14. *The remaining wing of Sir John Wollaston's house on The Bank, Highgate Hill. W. West redrew this scene from an early 19th century engraving  at a time when it was thought that the 16th century structure was part of Arundel House, which is now known to have been on the site of the Old Hall in South Grove. The building shown is, in fact, that occupied by Sir John Wollaston in the 17th century when he bought the manor of Hornsey during the Interregnum. Dr Benjamin Duncan's Commercial Academy is first noted here in 1813 but was gone by 1828 when the building appears to have been demolished. The whole site shown in this view is now occupied by Channing School.*

ARUNDEL HOUSE
THE BANK, HIGHGATE, 1810.

rebuilt, with funds supplied by Edward Pauncefort, as a row of twelve in *c*1726: it is these buildings which now survive, hemmed in by heavy traffic and Highgate School.

## NEIGHBOURS AT WAR

The Civil War found a number of Highgate residents at odds with each other. It was not a time for people to hide their convictions and Highgate neighbours found their fortunes shifting with those of the War itself. For example, Sir James Harrington, who lived in a large house in Highgate West Hill was one of judges at the trial of Charles I; he had to leave the country altogether at the Restoration. John Bill jnr, who lived at what became Kenwood House, was a Royalist and was imprisoned for his views. There is some evidence that Andrew Marvell, a vehement pro-Parliamentary supporter, lived in a cottage next door to his opponent, the Earl of Lauderdale.

A notable resident was Dr Elisha Coysh. He lived in a cottage in Swains Lane and rose to fame for his ability to treat victims of the Great Plague of 1665. One local historian has him aiding the escape of people fleeing from the plague, even hiding them at Highgate, so that they could later proceed north.

15. *Andrew Marvell*, (1621–78), from an oil painting by Hanneman. It was a strongly held tradition that Marvell the poet and Parliamentarian lived in the cottage next to Lauderdale House, depicted in *Illustration 17*.

16. *The Wollaston-Pauncefort Almshouses, Southwood Lane*, in 1877. Sir John Wollaston built six almshouses here in the 17th century, vested in Highgate School.
They were rebuilt as a row of twelve with a schoolmistress's house, by Sir Edward Pauncefort, who lived in Lauderdale House.

17. *Andrew Marvell's Cottage, Highgate Hill.* **This cottage stood next to Lauderdale House, further up the hill. The Hearth Tax** records for the period of Marvell's alleged residence show someone else as occupant, but this in itself does not disprove the tradition. Marvell in a letter written in 1675 says 'Being resolved now to sequester myself one whole Day at Highgate…' The cottage was demolished by Waterlow in 1867. A table, allegedly Marvell's, was presented to the Highgate Literary and Scientific Institution but, sadly, was stolen from there in 1977.

18. *William Murray, 1st Earl of Mansfield.* Engraving from a painting by Sir Joshua Reynolds.

19. *Kenwood House.* The north front in 1788, showing the walled courtyard and Hampstead Lane then running close by the front of the house. The Lane was diverted by the 2nd Earl so as to give him a larger front garden.

# Kenwood

### AN ANCIENT ESTATE

In Kenwood House is an 18th century painting, attributed to Richard Wilson, of a view from the terrace over London. No such vista exists today because a panoply of trees now intrudes. Robert Adam, who remodelled the house in the 18th century, describes 'a noble view let into the house and terrace, of the City of London, Greenwich Hospital and the river Thames, the ships passing up and down, with an extensive prospect, but clear and distinct, on both sides of the river.' Still, in the early 19th century, the Earl of Mansfield could look from his rear window across his own woods and pastures down to Mansfield Road in Gospel Oak, and see London beneath him.

Much earlier than the creation of this gentleman's retreat the forest of Middlesex covered the ground instead and stretched northwards beyond it. The Kenwood estate can be traced back to 1226 when it was owned by William de Blemont, of the family which gave its name to Bloomsbury. Held by a reli-

gious house until the Dissolution it was then disposed of by the Crown. In 1616 John Bill, the King's printer, bought the land and here built the first house, traces of which may still be found in the basement of the present classical building.

In 1754 the house and grounds were sold to its most famous owner, William Murray, then Attorney General and later to be Lord Chief Justice and Earl Mansfield. Murray was Scots, and he employed a Scottish architect, Robert Adam, to remodel and reface his country house. As Mansfield got older he spent more and more time here and it was at Kenwood, in 1793, that he died.

Robert Adam's work here was at its most inventive. The orangery already existed in the old house and Adam counterbalanced its shape at the other end of the house with the magnificent library. The centre, south facing, block was raised a storey and the whole refaced to present the aspect which, even after many sightings, still astounds one when it is seen from the distance. In the grounds the famous sham bridge over one of the lakes, beloved of those who watch concerts there, was introduced.

The second Earl made many changes. An important improvement concerned Hampstead Lane which at that time, following an old parish boundary, was very close to the front entrance to the house. Such intimacy with the general public was, of course, undesirable and the Earl was permitted to divert the road in a broad arc across land of the Bishop of London (which he also tenanted) to give him a large front garden and the privacy he wanted. With the extra space at the front it was possible then to introduce the two projecting wings on either side of the portico. The service wing, discreetly hidden by the rise of the land, containing kitchens, brewhouse, laundry and quarters, is also of this period. It is thought that Humphry Repton was brought in to advise on the further landscaping of the grounds.

Very little changed at Kenwood between that time and the 1st World War, but developments had happened on the associated farmland. Parliament Hill had long been coveted by developers and preservation groups alike and after much campaigning and persuasion the southern lands belonging to Mansfield (as well as the East Heath Park estate in Hampstead) were bought for the public and added to the Heath. But this still left Kenwood lands to the north, between Parliament Hill, and south of the present enclosed grounds below the house. Another public campaign managed to buy this land by 1924 but the house and its 76 acres were still out of reach and seemingly beyond the public pocket.

By 1922 the sixth Earl had sold the contents of the house (to the chagrin of curators since, who have struggled to bring back the items dispersed) and had drawn up plans for the building of 33 villas on the

grounds. All appeared lost until Lord Iveagh, former chairman of the Guinness brewery, bought the house and the remainder of the grounds for £108,000. These, and his own collection of paintings which he installed in the house, he left to the public in 1927. This magnificent and generous gift was opened to the public in 1928.

*20. The Earl of Mansfield's, at Caen Wood, near Hampstead, Middlesex.* Published in 1792. The illustration depicts the house with the road still close to the front and before the 2nd Earl built two wings projecting from the front of the house.

**KENWOOD HAMPSTEAD
LORD MANSFIELD
ROBERT ADAM 1767**
SITE PLAN SHOWS ORIGINAL DISPOSITION.
FROM A SURVEY MADE 1793, BYE
PRITCHARD. NOW IN THE CRACE
COLLECTION.
THE NEW LAY OUT MADE FOR
THE SECOND EARL OF
MANSFIELD BETWEEN 1793-97.

**KENWOOD**
ENLARGED PLAN OF THE HOUSE
FROM PLAN IN ADAM'S WORKS
CORRECTED WITH THE LATER
ADDITIONS

SCALE FOR HOUSE PLAN

SCALE FOR SITE PLAN

21. A plan of Kenwood, showing the building stages and a plan of the house. From a survey made in 1793.

22. A religious sect led by Thomas Venner, the Fifth Monarchy Men, mounted an unsuccessful insurrection in the City in 1661. In some confusion they retreated to the cover of Kenwood for a while and were later captured when once again they tried to attack the City.

*This Helmet was a Crown by Revelation
This Halbert was a Scepter for the Nation.
So the Fifth-Monarchy anew is grac'd
King Venner next to Iohn aLeydon plac'd .*

23. *A View of Kenwood*. Kenwood House from the rear, by G. Robertson in 1781. Humphry Repton was still to do his landscaping.

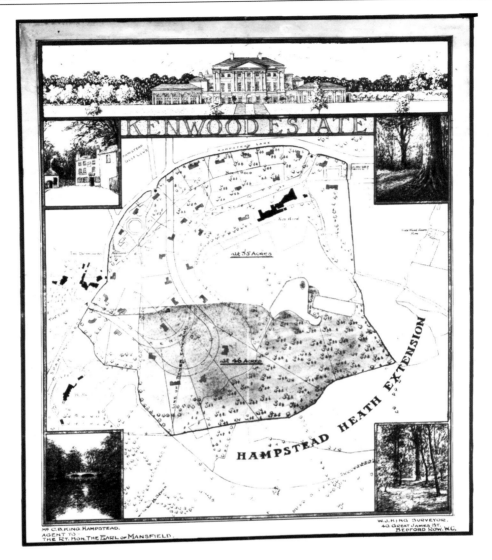

24. *Plan for building on the Kenwood Estate.* This scheme was published *c*1923 at a time when conservationist groups were struggling to find funds to buy the property for the public. The agent for the sale was C.B. King, a prominent Hampstead building firm.

25. *(Facing top) Long horned cattle at Kenwood.* by J.C. Ibbetson, 1797.

26. *(Facing bottom) Kenwood House.* From a drawing by A.R. Quinton, published in Barratt's *Annals of Hampstead*, (1912).

*View of Highgate, from the great Road at Kentish Town. | Vûe de Highgate, du Coté du grand Chemin à la Ville Kentish.*

27. *The parish map of St Pancras, Highgate section.* This map was commissioned by St Pancras Vestry. It is the first large scale map of the parish and compared to present-day Ordnance Survey plans it is quite accurate. It was begun by John Prickett, surveyor of Highgate, and completed by John Thompson between 1796 and 1800.

28. *A View of Highgate from the great Road at Kentish Town.* This view by Chatelain, published in 1752, was taken from Highgate Road, probably near to Swains Lane. Most likely the building in the centre with the cupola is Cromwell House.

# Village to Town

### THE TOWN MAP

The first clear map of much of Highgate was made in the 1790s. It was begun by John Prickett, surveyor of Highgate, whose descendants founded Prickett and Ellis, estate agents, and was completed by John Thompson. It is a mine of information. In fact, Prickett's survey was of the whole of the St Pancras parish on four sheets, and *Illustration 27* is merely the Highgate section. Unfortunately, as Prickett was being paid by St Pancras Vestry, he excluded buildings on the other side of the High Street.

His map should be looked at together with two contemporary drawings (*Illustrations 29* and *30*) which depict Pond Square, for these add dimension to the shapes on the map.

29. *Pond Square from the south.* This illustration, *c*1790, depicts the two ponds with Rock House on the left. The Gatehouse tavern and the chapel are beyond the horse.

30. *Pond Square from the north..* This view, also of *c*1790, looks down Highgate High Street from outside the Gatehouse tavern. Church House is on the right.

It will be seen in *Illustration 29* that Pond Square still had its two ponds. Rock House (a name derived from an occupant in the 1840s) is shown on the left with some of the existing cottages in Pond Square backing on to it. In the range facing into the ponds two cottages exist in the illustration and on the map there are three or four. The top corner of the Square was then open and it was possible to see no. 47 Highgate West Hill, home of the village doctor from

1750, and, to the right of it, The Gatehouse pub.

The view facing the reverse direction across Pond Square, *Illustration 30*, shows Church House prominently to the right, ·fronted by a high wall; unfortunately the premises in which the Highgate Literary and Scientific Institution later took up residence are obscured by trees.

The small building with the triangular roof in the centre of the picture is the Highgate lock-up, a short-

term prison used until the prisoners could be handed over to the justices. It was described in 1820 as being 7 foot square, 6 feet high, and without any opening whatsoever, except for a grille presumably. Nearby, the little shops along the High Street were called Watch House Row, named from the placing of a watchman's headquarters in this terrace.

On the left hand side of the High Street, the Rose and Crown is in the foreground, but the second inn sign behind it is the only representation we have of a pub called the White Lion, at nos. 64–66, which in the 18th century was the most prominent place of entertainment in Highgate, with assemblies, balls and public meetings. It was closed in 1784 and unless the inn sign was left up for a few years, its depiction here would alter the usual dating of this illustration.

The houses in The Grove are named Quality Walk, a splendid name for estate agents to conjure with.

WILLIAM CUTBUSH & SON'S SEED SHOP, OFFICE, AND CONSERVATORY.

*31. The house and shop of William Cutbush, nurseryman, 80 Highgate West Hill.* Nos. 78–79 Highgate West Hill, probably built in the 16th century, are on the site of the White Hart Inn. In 1769 the house and its sloping gardens were owned by William Bowstread, market gardener, whose business was acquired in the early part of the 19th century by the aptly named William Cutbush. In 1834 Cutbush built the house and shop depicted above and by 1871 the nursery employed 25 people.

Ashurst House may be seen, then in the possession of Thomas Walker, on the site of St Michael's Church; Lauderdale House is on the far right, then being used for Mrs Sheldon's private school.

Behind these are the fields and meadows which must have made Highgate at that time a spectacular place. Mr Bowstread is shown in possession of nos. 78–79 Highgate West Hill; his nursery garden, begun in 1769, was subsequently that of the splendidly named Cutbush & Son, whose horticultural skills were known all over London.

## MORE NEW MANSIONS

The only serious rival to the splendour of Kenwood House was nearby in Hampstead Lane. Where now stands the closely guarded Beechwood, a farmhouse called Sherricks existed in 1650. The land here (and, indeed, much more all the way down to Fitzrovia) passed by a profitable sleight of hand to the Fitzroy family in the 18th century. On the site of the old farmhouse Charles Fitzroy, the first Baron South-ampton, erected *c*1774 a sumptuous but short-lived mansion, Fitzroy House, with grounds laid out by 'Capability' Brown reached by a tree-lined driveway represented today by Fitzroy Park. The last tenant of this house, before it was demolished about 1826, was Henry Robarts, a banker, and his guests included Coleridge, Byron, Keats and Rogers.

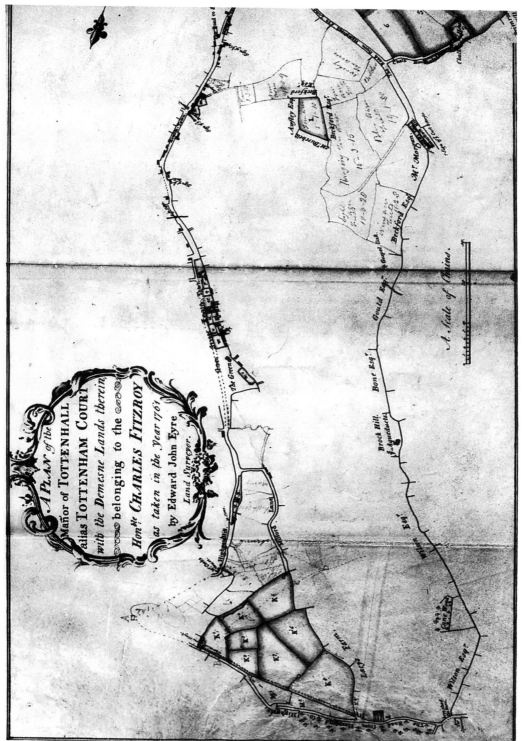

32. *A Plan of the Tottenhall alias Tottenham Court with the Demesne Lands therin belonging to the Hon[ble] Charles Fitzroy, as taken in the Year 1761 by Edward John Eyre, Land Surveyor.* (Section only). The Tottenhall manor stretched from Hampstead Lane to Fitzrovia. It was acquired very cheaply by Charles Fitzroy in the middle of the 18th century from St Paul's Cathedral. The top road is represented today by Highgate West Hill; to the left Millfield (Milford) Lane branches off up to Hampstead Lane and the Fitzroy residence. The boundary line at the bottom of the plan goes across Parliament Hill Fields.

*33. Lord Southampton's Lodge at Highgate, Middlesex*, published in 1792. This mansion, approximately on the site of today's Beechwood, did not last long. Erected in *c*1774, it was demolished about 1826. Its driveway is represented today by Fitzroy Park.

The bottom of the hill, too, had its mansion. It was more modest, but sufficient to push its owner into bankruptcy. It stood just south of Swains Lane in Highgate Road and it was built by a solicitor called Gregory Bateman of Maiden Lane, Covent Garden, in 1777. This house is shown on the dustjacket and in *Illustration 34*. The picture is of particular importance, not only because it has only once before been reproduced, but because it includes views of properties not otherwise portrayed.

Highgate West Hill winds away on the left of the picture and Swains Lane is, presumably, behind the hedge running to the right of the horseman. Behind that is a farmhouse on the site of St Anne's church, then occupied by Thomas Greenwood. To the far left is a house by the side of Highgate West Hill. It is difficult to be sure of its identity, but the most likely candidate is the residence in which Mary and William Howitt first lived in Highgate, which had an old

hermitage attached. Mary Howitt asserts that one of its earlier tenants was Sir Wallis Porter, a friend of the Prince Regent, and it was here that 'orgies' of a gambling kind were carried on, beneath a salaciously painted ceiling. To its right on the horizon, is a large house with three bays in 16th century style. In theory, judging from its position and the known buildings of the time, this ought to be Parkfield, a predecessor of Witanhurst, which we know was here in the 17th century. But the style does not match a photograph of the old house which shows it to be distinctly early 18th century. In the centre of the horizon the domed tower of Ashurst House may be seen and this is the only picture in which we have a side elevation of the building.

Another mystery remains – the large house to the far right of the hill's horizon. The most likely candidate is Cromwell House, but in that case it appears to be an inaccurate drawing.

*34. Kentish Town House.* This house, pictured in 1787, was at the top of Highgate Road just before Swains Lane. It was built by Gregory Bateman in 1777 in the style of Wanstead House, in Essex. He went bankrupt soon afterwards and his grand house lasted only until the late 1840s, when St Alban's Villas and Road were built on its site. Highgate West Hill leads off to the left.

## BUILDING UP THE HIGH STREET

New building was not confined to detached mansions. In the 18th century the High Street was upgraded as well. On The Bank, next to Cromwell House, Ireton House and Lyndale House were built as a single dwelling. Cholmeley Lodge replaced the old Mermaid Inn and the White House at no. 10 was substantially rebuilt. On the other side nos. 17–21, which were rebuilt in 1733, provided income to a charity established by Elizabeth Gould 'for the benefit of the poor inhabitants of the town and vill of Highgate'. These houses survive today as does too the slightly older and grander Englefield House at no. 23.

Over the years other houses on this stretch had increased in size. Fairseat was now quite substantial and so was Bisham House, which stood on the site of the avenue of that name. One of its residents was Captain Heywood, a seemingly reluctant mutineer against William Bligh on *HMS Bounty*.

Around the corner, in South Grove, Church House was built in the early 18th century and soon after was owned by Sir John Hawkins, a lawyer and a man described uncharitably by his contemporaries. He was a friend of Samuel Johnson and, indeed,

wrote a biography of the great man. Never could a book be so overshadowed by another! From 1802 Church House was a Jewish boys' boarding school.

*35. Nos. 17–21 Highgate High Street.* (1932). Houses were on this site by 1636 and were rebuilt in their present form *c*1733. They were the basis for a charity established by Elizabeth Gould for the poor people of the village.

*36. Cruchley's New Plan of London and its Environs.* This map shows the extent of change in much of Highgate since the plan shown in *Illustration 27*. It contains a number of street names, now gone. Pembroke Row, instead of South Grove, is probably a mistake, because The Grove was at one time called Pemberton Row, and it is possible that the map's compiler has got rather confused here. The High Street, as a name, continues up North Road, and Southwood Lane is Southgate Lane, probably also a mistake. It is interesting that the Archway Road is still referred to as Tunnel Road, although the plan to make a tunnel here had never been completed. The original plan was published in 1829 but it has been updated in this version insofar as the old Highgate Cemetery (1839) is included.

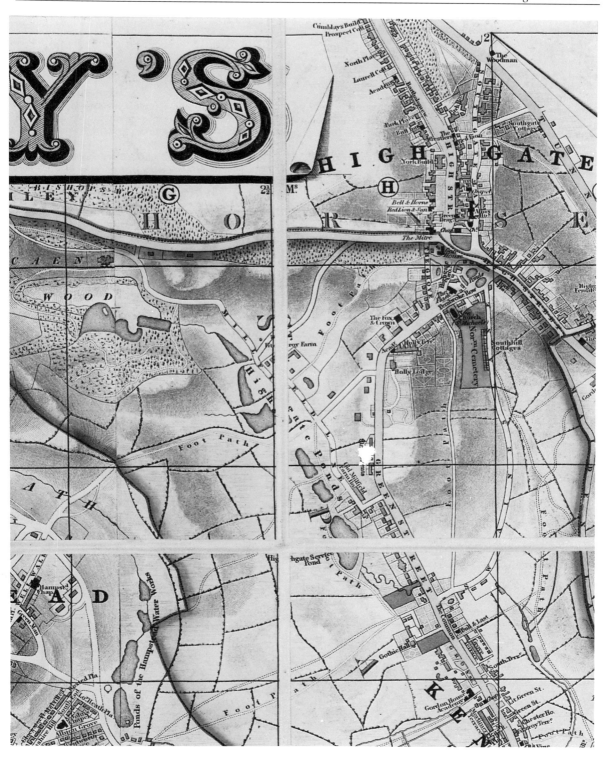

# Extraordinary People

*37. William Powell, Prophet of Highgate.* From an engraving published in 1804.

### THE PROPHET OF HIGHGATE

An eccentric sufficiently famed to have a print made of him (*Illustration 37*) was William Powell, who died in 1803, at the age of sixty-four. While working at the Treasury he was fortunate enough to win £500 on a lottery but this largesse encouraged him to neglect his work so that he had to resign. He lived in Sloane Street, Chelsea but every day, in all weathers, he walked early in the morning to the foot of Highgate Hill and then, raising his hand as if in devotion, started up in a run and never stopped or looked back until he reached the top of the hill. If he were hindered anywhere along the route, he would return to the bottom and try again. When asked why he did this he asserted that when he ceased the world would be no more.

WILLIAM POWELL,
*Parry del.*  *The Highgate Prophet &c.*  *A. Van Assen sc.*

# A CONTROVERSIAL CLERIC

Religious fundamentalism was to the fore in England at the beginning of the 18th century. Best known of the political preachers of the time was Dr Henry Sacheverell, scourge of the low church, dissenters, Whigs and foreigners. In 1709 he preached two sermons, one at Derby, the other at St Paul's, both of which were violent in their language, and which strongly attacked the prevailing government tendency towards religious toleration. His words were judged by the House of Commons to be 'malicious, scandalous and seditious libels, highly reflecting upon Her Majesty and her government, the late happy revolution, and the protestant succession.' As a result Sacheverell was impeached, to the fury of a sympathetic public opinion. The Whigs insisted that a show trial should take place in Westminster Hall and when Sacheverell drove to his hearing a multitude of people went with him and riots had to be quelled. He was found guilty, given a nominal sentence and his sermons were burnt by the common hangman, but it was generally recognised that Sacheverell and the high church had won the day.

His connection with Highgate is that some years after, by then loaded with honours and rich from an inheritance and a fortuitous marriage, he took up residence in South Grove House, on the site of today's block of flats, and here he died in 1724.

In 1759 Thomas Bromwich, a paper merchant of Ludgate Hill, bought this house. His fortune had principally derived from inventing a wallpaper which imitated stucco work. He died a rich man in 1787 and two years later his widow, then nearly 80, scandalised everyone by marrying her coachman, in his twenties. The *Gentleman's Magazine* reported in the uncompromising way of the time when noting her marriage:

'Sept 13. At St Pancras Church, Mrs Bromwich, of Highgate, aged near 80, to her coachman, James Wheeler, a stout young man, aged about 25. She was the widow of the late Mr B., a paper machée manufacturer on Ludgate Hill...She possessed near £1000 per annum. Her children, some time since, offered Mr. W. £500 if he would quit her service, and afterwards £400 a year, both of which he refused, conceiving the whole property better than a part, which the lady generously gave him on condition of taking her person into the bargain. This is the fourth time the above lady has been married.'

*38. Dr. Henry Sacheverell, (1674–1724), who lived at South Grove House.*

## COLERIDGE AT HIGHGATE

In middle age Samuel Taylor Coleridge, the poet, was addicted to laudanum, a tincture of opium. Originally he had dosed himself to relieve head pains but by the age of 24 he admitted himself addicted and a few years later wrote of the 'pleasurable sensations' opium brought, and *Kubla Khan* appears to have been written under its influence. From a combination of the damage the drug caused to his health and a despondency over a lack of money and popular literary success, he was at a low ebb when Dr James Gillman, who then lived at Moreton House in South Grove, was persuaded to take Coleridge into his care. The poet lived with the family from 1816 and moved with them to no. 3 The Grove in 1823. Here the Gillmans patiently looked after him, establishing a routine in his life and easing him away from dependency on opium, although it is not clear if that ever disappeared. But Coleridge was gregarious and talkative enough and many friends came to see him in Highgate, including Lamb, Keats, Wordsworth (with whom he was particularly friendly) and Frederick Denison Maurice whose Christian Socialism Coleridge flirted with for a time.

Coleridge died in Highgate in 1834 and was buried in Highgate Old Chapel; his remains were transferred to St Michael's in 1961.

BACK VIEW OF M^R GILLMAN'S HOUSE AT HIGHGATE, 1833.

COLERIDGE OCCUPIED TOP ROOM ON RIGHT.

W. WEST.

N° 39

# A FOUNDER OF MANY THINGS

In the days when a wealthy person with a social conscience could make a significant impact on an area, Harry Chester had a hand in quite a few Highgate ventures.

Chester, whose father Sir Robert lived in the Old Hall, married Anna Maria Isherwood and lived at South Grove House, which had been owned by the Isherwood family. He was Secretary to the Permanent Committee on Education of the Privy Council and his interests lay in the national reform of educational availability and teaching.

Chester was founder of the Highgate Literary and Scientific Institution in 1839; in 1847, together with two other residents, he leased six acres off Hampstead Lane so that the landless of Highgate could cultivate allotments; in 1852 his particular project, St Michael's Schools in North Road, were opened. He and the vicar were also responsible for persuading Highgate shopkeepers (many of them reluctant converts) to stop trading on Sundays. In addition he was a Governor of Highgate School and, for a time, its Treasurer. Lloyd, in his *History of Highgate* mentions that Chester had a more ancient connection with Highgate insofar as an ancestor was Sir Julius Caesar (a Muswell Hill resident and friend of the 2nd Earl of Arundel). It was in Caesar's arms that Francis Bacon died at Arundel House in South Grove in 1626.

*39. (Facing top) Samuel Taylor Coleridge.* From a painting by Washington Allston, 1814.

*40. (Facing bottom) The Back View of Mr Gillman's house at Highgate, 1833.* This is the rear of no. 3 The Grove, where Coleridge lived from 1823 until his death

*41. Harry Chester.*

# A Road Through the Hill

## THE FIRST ATTEMPT

It is difficult today to imagine Highgate without the Archway Road, or at least a road on that line. But it has to be remembered that the ridge of land behind the back gardens of Cromwell House and its neighbours on either side of the Hornsey Lane, extended across the route of the present road and that the Lane itself was a path over that ridge. The long, sometimes impossible, haul up Highgate Hill from Holloway Road was sufficient reason for plans to cut through the land mass.

*42. The Seal of the Highgate Archway Company 1810.* This depicts traffic labouring up Highgate Hill and cantering through a mean looking tunnel – the latter, of course, was never built.

*43. (Below) Highgate Archway.* An engraving by J. and H.S. Storer, *c*1820.

*44. (Facing) The old Highgate Archway.*

It was a Cornish mining engineer, Robert Vaizey, who came up with the first considered plan to join Holloway Road to the Great North Road; it consisted of a long tunnel and much of the rest in a cutting. Inside, the tunnel was arched, and this was the derivation of the 'archway' term.

Work began despite protest from those residents about to lose their back gardens, and innkeepers in the village who expected to lose trade, and there was much rejoicing when, in the early hours of 13 April 1812, the tunnel collapsed before completion. Fortunately, no-one was in it at the time. The workmen themselves had foretold the catastrophe, pointing out an economy in the use of bricks and quality of cement.

## A SECOND TRY

The promoters then reverted to the original advice of John Rennie, the celebrated engineer, who thought that the road should be entirely in a cutting, with a bridge supporting Hornsey Lane. It would cost far more but there was no alternative really, because travellers would hardly have trusted a replacement tunnel. The new bridge, held up by an elongated archway and three smaller ones above it, designed by John Nash, was opened in 1813.

The promoters' worries were not over, however. The road was not a success, either because the tolls were unwelcome or else the surface was poor, and it was not until the 1830s that their fortunes improved. The road was paid for eventually, not from the tolls, but from the sale of spare agricultural land for building purposes.

The archway devised by Nash was a narrow one, although not so restrictive as most prints suggest. It was 18 feet wide but increased traffic would, eventually, have done for it. The most pressing reason for its replacement was the building of a tramway and in 1894 the London County Council obtained powers to build the present wide-span bridge, designed by Sir Alexander Binnie, which was opened in 1900.

*45. The Woodman, Archway Road.* The building of the Archway Road brought about the construction of at least three public houses – the Archway Tavern, the Wellington (closed recently) and the Woodman, pictured here in the 1880s. Archway Road crosses left to right and the road to Muswell Hill is beyond.

46. *View of Highgate Archway.* From an aquatint by J. Hill of a picture by A. Pugin, published in August 1812. In fact, the road was not opened until August the following year and this is presumably an imagined view of the traffic to come. This probably explains the lack of a tollgate, seen in all other prints of this period. The Archway Tavern, at the junction of Archway Road and Highgate Hill, is not yet built. The castellated building to the left is College House Academy (see also *Illustration 118*).

# THE WHITTINGTON ALMSHOUSES

One early occupant of the Archway Road, possibly the first, was the Whittington Almshouses. This institution, founded in 1424 by a bequest of Richard Whittington, in the City, moved here *c*1824 to pleasant and picturesque quarters, although the occupants must have felt decidedly isolated. It is odd that the Mercers' Company, who administered the almshouses, should have built them near the place where the *legendary* Whittington is said to have made his famous about-turn from the slopes of Highgate back to the City and fortune. The buildings, designed by George Smith, housed 24 old single women and a cleric. They were pulled down in 1967 to effect a widening of the road, and instead of the charming view the almshouses once gave us we have an unattractive mess.

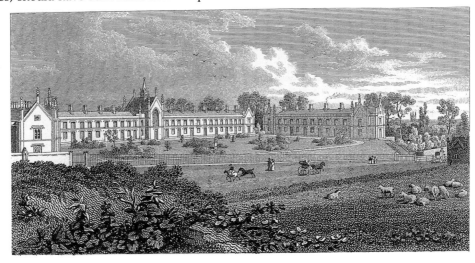

47.  *Whittington College*. Whittington Almshouses, built *c*1824 are here depicted *c*1835. The tollgate to the Archway Road is far right.

48.  *Brickfields, Archway Road*. It was fortunate for the promoters of the Archway Road, who had seen little return on their money, that the surplus land purchased turned out to be productive brickfields, as shown in this *c*1880 photograph. Holborn Infirmary, later the Archway Wing of Whittington Hospital, is in the distance, and to its left is the old tollgate and Whittington Almshouses.

# On the Other Side of the Hill

After the Restoration in 1660 the manor of Hornsey reverted to its previous owner, the Bishop of London. His estate stretched from the north side of the High Street to Friern Barnet, and from Finsbury Park (then called Hornsey Wood) to a medieval building on the site of one of the links of Highgate Golf Course, called Bishop's Lodge. This structure appears to have been a hunting lodge surrounded by a moat, and it is still possible to see its lines, although it has not been excavated. It was probably built in Norman

times and demolished in the late 14th century.

Southwood Lane contained most of the development on this side of the hill other than houses in the High Street. The whole length of this lane, up to Muswell Hill, was called Southwood Lane, and only in the 1880s was the stretch past Archway Road called Muswell Hill Road.

Five substantial houses were on the eastern side of the road, of which two survive – Southwood Lodge, tucked away in the new Kingsley Place development, and The Limes, more recently the Southwood Hospital. Two other large houses were on the site of the Southwood Park apartment blocks. Southwood

*49. Sketch Map of The Bishop of London's Manor of Hornsey.* This map, compiled by W. McBeath Marcham and Frank Marcham, was published in their book entitled *Court Rolls of the Bishop of London's Manor of Hornsey 1603–1701*, in 1929. It is designed to locate the various field names and features mentioned in the court rolls of the period.

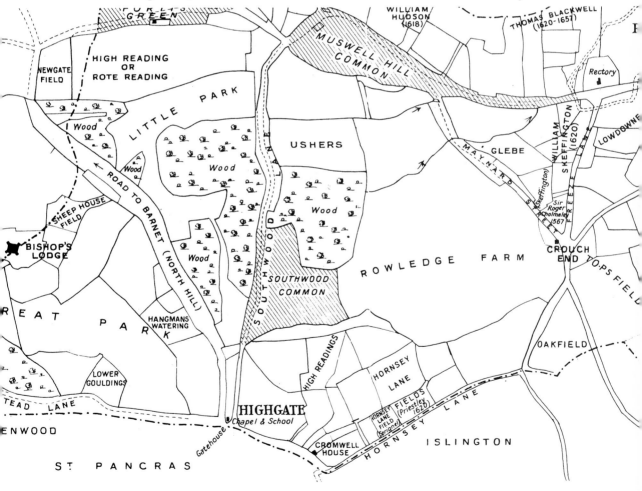

*50. Hornsey Enclosure Map, 1819. (Highgate section)* This map was produced to show the extent of the manorial holdings

*51. The grounds of Southwood.* This house can be traced back to at least 1707, but this view is of the 1840s when it had an uninterrupted view of the valley beyond it. It was demolished in the 1930s.

*52. The garden front of Hillside.* Hillside is the house in Jackson's Lane which overhangs the road. An early occupier was Joseph Jackson, from whom the road derived its name, and a later resident was John Lloyd from whose book, *The History of Highgate* (1888), this illustration is taken.

(there are many variations of Southwood to contend with!) may be traced to 1707. In 1839 it was owned by Mark Beauchamp Peacock, solicitor to the Post Office, who considerably enlarged it. It was demolished by Lord Southwood in 1934 so that he could enlarge the garden of his own house, Southwood Court. His house, a much newer property, was on the corner with Southwood Lawn Road. Its chimney piece was emblazoned with the arms of John Grove Johnson, assayer to the Bank of England, and on demolition, these were removed and inset into the Southwood Lane blocks.

Southwood House stood between Jackson's Lane and Hillside Gardens. It was demolished in the late 1950s and flats and houses built on the site. It was built in about 1746 on the site of an earlier residence of Field Marshal George Wade who was renowned for his expertise in building roads for military purposes, but who had little success when it came to winning battles. Two granite posts near this estate by the roadside mark the site of wells.

Along what became Jackson's Lane Southwood Lawn was built by 1746, and Hillside, one-time home of historian John Lloyd, was erected about the same time. It is difficult to be certain of the date of Bank Point, which clings precariously to the triangle bounded by Southwood and Jackson's Lane, but there is record of it by 1816.

# The Institution

## A MODEST START

A hundred and fifty years ago, in January 1839, a gathering of local worthies at the Gatehouse Tavern resolved to form an institution in the village 'to excite and cultivate an intelligent interest in the objects of literature and science.' The Highgate Literary and Scientific Institution was born.

It was the busy era after the 1832 Reform Act, a period alive with good intentions and resolutions that, nevertheless, were mostly unattained for generations. However, throughout the country, numerous similar institutions were founded. In most towns the middle classes and the superior tradesmen put their names and subscriptions up and in many cases quite impressive premises were built. Nearby, for

example, the Islington organisation opened the splendid building off Upper Street now used by the Almeida Theatre, and on the site of the petrol station opposite Holloway Prison the Camden Athenaeum opened in a suitably classical building.

In contrast in Highgate, with its greater prosperity and its more closely woven society, its Institution struggled to make ends meet. After a year it moved out of two rooms in Southwood Lane to the outbuildings and stables attached to Church House in South Grove, and although some work was done in converting these premises the Institution was in a parlous state by 1874, sufficiently depleted in membership and funds to instruct its secretary to wind it up.

For legal reasons it was not possible to withdraw from the lease until 1881 and in the meantime a new secretary was appointed – John Lloyd, whose history of Highgate, published in 1888, has been a much-loved standard work since. He and others put new zest into the place and there was even a proposal, opposed by local residents, to erect a new building on Pond Square once the ponds had been drained.

53. *The Highgate Literary and Scientific Institution.* A photograph taken in 1964.

## NEW ENERGY

The Institution's subsequent history could hardly have been predicted. It is not only the last surviving such establishment in the London area but, in a modest way, it is flourishing in the 1980s. Even now it is in the throes of a substantial programme of improvements to widen its appeal to new generations of Highgate residents.

The Institution embodies the unusual, at least for London, character of Highgate. Despite the traffic, the horrendous rise in house prices, the loss of useful shops and all the other factors which destroy a close-bound community, the village and the Institution remain neighbourly, gossipy, and still not entirely in

the 20th century let alone near the end of it. People like Lloyd, or the Institution's founder, the educational reformer, Harry Chester, would feel at home in the building and familiar with the activities, which remain true to the principles first adopted.

Without doubt part of the reason for the Institution's survival has been the library. On the fringes of three boroughs the main village has been neglected by each of them in terms of library provision. The Institution has met much of that need and the library's character has been forged in more recent times by the appointment as librarian of Elaine Vaughan in 1939 and then by her daughter Gwynydd Gosling, who is still there today.

*54. The interior of the library at the Highgate Literary and Scientific Institution.* This 1895 photograph shows the librarians, Mr and Mrs H. Holt.

CHOLMELEY SCHOOL AND HIGHGATE CHAPEL,
REMOVED 1833.

W.WEST.

*55. Cholmeley School and Highgate Chapel.* This redrawing by W. West of an old print, shows the school building and the old chapel, which was demolished in 1833.

# Highgate School

## SIR ROGER CHOLMELEY'S BEQUEST

The 16th century saw many schools founded. There were several practical ways by which wealthy people could hope to merit the benefits of heaven – they could leave money for regular prayers to be offered for their souls, or they could found almshouses, chapels or schools. Sir Roger Cholmeley, one of the largest landowners in Highgate, chose education.

Cholmeley lived in a house on the site of Fairseat in the High Street. He also farmed the fields which are now Waterlow Park, and others in the neighbourhood of The Grove, Highgate West Hill and Crouch End. In 1552 he was Lord Chief Justice. But such was the nature of the times he was in the Tower the following year, for having witnessed the will of Edward VI, which sought to exclude Mary from the throne. Cholmeley saved his neck by accepting the new queen, but he faded from public life and retired to Highgate. It was in his house in the village, in 1555, that the future Queen Elizabeth I stayed for one night on her way to court.

Cholmeley seems to have acquired the property on which stood the old hermitage chapel in 1562 and to have applied for permission to found his school there the same year. Letters patent were granted in 1565, just before his death. The school probably opened in 1571 and the intention was to teach forty poor children from Highgate, Holloway, Hornsey, Finchley and Kentish Town virtually free of charge. In exchange the pupils were required to be 'at seven of the clock in the morning…devoutly upon their knees' at prayer.

Cholmeley's school was, in most respects, a conventional charity grammar school of the time. Most likely it would have faded into oblivion once church and state schools came into prominence, but because of the persistence of one man, it didn't.

*56. (Above) View of Highgate School and Chapel.* Watercolour by George Varley, 1828.

*57. (Facing) Highgate scholars at Elgin House.* As the number of pupils at Highgate school increased under the headship of J. Bradley Dyne extra space had to be found in outside buildings. Elgin House at no. 2 High Street is shown in the 1851 census to have 17 boys boarding. This photograph was taken in 1865.

## CHAPEL OR SCHOOL?

As has been mentioned earlier *(page 12)* the School's chapel was an important feature in the village. The old hermitage had acted as a chapel-of-ease before the foundation of the School and this function continued with the blessing of the School governors. The chapel registers show that it was used increasingly for those events that mark people's lives, and its administration was more profitable than that of the School. The headmaster, who was also Reader at the chapel, could be excused for neglecting his charity pupils for the gentry who occupied his pews, and certainly the governors had no objection. Things got so lax that a House of Commons report in 1819 noted that the forty boys were actually taught by the sexton (a parish official, himself usually poor and illiterate). The master said that he did not teach them because he was too taken up with his pastoral work!

Matters came to a head in the 1820s. The position was reached that either the old chapel should be enlarged to cope with Highgate's increased population or else it should be restricted to the use of the School, leaving the parishioners to their own devices. This begged the question: To whom did the chapel really belong, the churchwardens representing the parish, or the governors representing the School?

Lord Eldon, then Lord High Chancellor, heard a great deal of evidence from both sides in this contentious matter and finally delivered a judgement in 1827 which pronounced that the chapel belonged to the charity which ran the School. That charity was intended for the teaching of learned languages and the governors were not bound to enlarge the chapel, or indeed to do anything for the benefit of the other inhabitants of Highgate. This verdict led to the opening of St Michael's Church in South Grove in 1832. At last Highgate residents had their own church and the next year a National School connected with it was built.

This did not improve the nature of Highgate school however. When the Rev Samuel Mence, schoolmaster and vicar of the new St Michael's, retired in 1838, there were only 19 boys in the school. In the changed circumstances this situation could well have ended in the winding-up of Cholmeley's charity. But it didn't.

Elgin House.

Nov. 1865.

2    1
3
4    5  6  7
8

21 20 19 18 17 16 15 14 13 12 11 10 9      22
23 24 25

| | | | |
|---|---|---|---|
| 1. A.M.Rendell Esq. | 6. C.Armstrong | 11. W.S.Scrimgeour. | 16. F.A.B.Sewell. | 21. W.O.Rew. |
| 2. E.P.Evans | 7. W.J.Law. | 12. S.Hebert | 17. T.C.Porter. | 22. G.O.Jackson |
| 3. A.E.Pole | 8. G.F.H.Blaydes. | 13. P.H.Marriott. | 18. F.M.Baker | 23. V.E.Knocker |
| 4. A.W.Hanson | 9. H.R.C.Smith | 14. E.J.Hebert | 19. W.J.Garrett | 24. H.A.Towse. |
| 5. A.W.Lloyd. | 10. C.W.Hughes | 15. C.Hall. | 20. J.H.Baker. | 25. W.Browne. |

## TRANSFORMATION

The next headmaster was John Bradley Dyne, son of a Somerset lawyer. Under him the School expanded its fee-paying numbers which, by then, it was allowed to do. By 1865 the School still had its forty free scholars, but it had ninety paying pupils as well and this trend continued as the School's reputation increased and the local well-to-do families saw it as a convenient stepping-stone to university. Dyne enlarged the School, adding boarding houses, sports fields and a library. He also acquired Cholmeley House in Southwood Lane, where Dyne House stands. Some of the hotch-potch of shops on the school side of North Road were taken down and a rebuilding of the School took place. The central block was opened in 1866 and the present chapel, designed by F.P. Cockerell, was consecrated the following year. Some large boarding houses were built in Broadlands Road and in 1879 the freeholds of several large houses in Bishopswood Road were bought; throughout this time the School increased its playing field areas along Hampstead Lane, buying up the working men's allotments on the way. When Dyne retired in 1874 he left the old charity as an established English public school.

Celebrated old boys include Gerard Manley Hopkins, John Betjeman, Anthony Crosland, Sir Clive Sinclair, and old masters include T.S. Eliot.

*58. A Highgate School staff group, 1869.*

Sept: 1869.

Rev. W.D. Bodkin.  G. Black.  E. Bickersteth. H.R.C. Smith.

C.H. Gardner Esq. Rev. R.L. Morris Rev. A.M. Rendell. Rev. R. Fletcher. H.A. Dalton. E. Miller Esq.  A.J. Leach.

W.L.A. Bartlett.  W. Scrimgeour. C.G. Church.

*59. View of Highgate Chapel and Schoolhouse, 1784.*

*60. The Old Library, Highgate School.* Postcard, *c*1910.

## A SCHOOLBOY'S LIFE

The rules of the School, drawn up in 1571, governed the scholar's life. Rule 5 said 'Acknowledging God to be the author of all knowledge, learning, and virtue, we order that the said master of this free school, with the scholars, at seven of the clock every morning, do, devoutly kneeling upon their knees , pray to Almighty God…' Next, 'And after prayers, he [the master] do remain in the school, diligently teaching, reading, and interpreting, or writing till eleven in the forenoon, and not to depart but upon very urgent and great causes.' Later, 'We order, that by one of the clock after dinner he do resort to the school again, there to remain with the scholars, till five or six of the clock of the night, according to the time of the year…'

C.A. Evors in his *The Story of Highgate School* assumes that the curriculum would have been grammar, Latin and the three R's, with no more than twenty days holiday a year. The boys would have dressed in padded doublets, with trunk hose puffed out and slashed above the middle of the thigh, broad shoes, flat caps, and a stiff ruffle round the neck.

In the 1880s the School fees were £24 per annum for tuition and £60 for boarding. Extra term expenses were piano lessons at 2 guineas, the gymnasium cost £1 and the swimming bath 50p.

## HIGHGATE SCHOOL.

Third Term 19 33.

Name Glassborow DW.

Final Place 14 in M Sc Form.

| SUBJECTS OF STUDY. | RANK IN FORM. | NUMBER OF BOYS IN FORM. | AVERAGE AGE OF BOYS. | REPORT. |
|---|---|---|---|---|
| English History | 22 | 23 | 15-6½ | Bad during early part of term; has improved |
| English Literature | 6 | 23 | 15-6½ | Has ability and should do well. |
| Geography | 12 | 15 | 15-7½ | F. |
| Divinity | 13 | 15 | 15-7½ | M. |
| French | 3 | 23 | 15-6½ | Good knowledge of Iren |
| German | | | | |
| Latin ML 2B. | 6 | 30 | 15-6 | Promising, if he would bestir himself. |
| Chemistry | 23 | 23 | 15-6½ | Has found these subjects difficult, but the Exam results show that he has been steadily progre |
| Physics | 20 | 23 | 15-6½ | |
| Mathematics DIVISION U iv A . | 2 | 25 | 15-10 | V. g., but untidy. |

| Book-keeping | | Shorthand |
|---|---|---|
| Drawing | Music — Vocal | Instrumental |

Form Master's General Report Has made a good commencer appears lethargic at times, & I he could do better if he put more energy into his b

House Tutor's Report A sound boy who will do well with more experience. Something should be done about his handwriting.

*Jass Johnston* HEAD MASTER.

*S. P. Kipping.* FORM MASTER.

*A C Kay.* HOUSE TUTOR.

N.B.   G—Good.   F—Fair.   M—Moderate.   B—Bad.   V—Very.

Holiday Work Galsworthy: " The Man of Property " .

Next Term begins Jan. 19th , ends March 29th

Boarders return Jan. 18th , not later than 8 p.m.

*Every Boy must appear punctually on the appointed day, exc case of illness, or some urgent reason to be notified beforehand by letter Head Master.*

61. *The School Report, 1933. of D.W. Glassborow.*
(Reproduced by kind permission of the scholar).

62. *Army cadets in Highgate School quadrangle, 1894.*

63. *Highgate School from the road.*

*64. Highgate Schoolboys in the quadrangle.*

*65. Highgate Schoolboys crossing Southwood Lane.* This photograph taken *c*1955 is a reminder of the days when traffic at the top end of Southwood Lane was two-way.

# A Place for Drinking

## EARLY PUBS

The earliest pub we know of in Highgate is the Swan, mentioned in 1480; it was, most likely, on the south side of the High Street but it is impossible to be sure. A 'Cornerhouse' on the site of today's Angel contained a brewery by the end of the 15th century and as there were five inns in the village by 1552 we can only assume that a number of the older pubs, including the Angel, go back that far.

Highgate's role as a victualling place, particularly for those going to Smithfield and the City, brought about a disproportionate number of inns and alehouses in the village. (By 1841 there were 21 public houses in Highgate and only about 700 adult males noted in the census returns.).

Some of the older establishments have disappeared. The Mermaid, for example, on the site of the Cholmeley Lodge flats occurs in the court rolls of 1624. The Black Dog, on the site of St Joseph's Retreat, was reputed to be 300 years old when it was bought for religious use in 1858. The Red Lion, at no. 90 North Road, was there by 1664 and closed in 1900. The Cow and Hare at the foot of Highgate West Hill, the site of St Anne's church, was trading by 1694 and the Fox and Crown whose landlord attained fame by halting a runaway coach containing the young Queen Victoria, was open at no. 40 Highgate West Hill by· 1704. This last named pub, demolished in 1898, sported a coat-of-arms after the royal rescue, and this is now proudly displayed in the Highgate Literary and Scientific Institution.

66. *The Angel, Highgate High Street, 1882.* The old building has been heavily 'Tudorised' – a fate which also befell the Gatehouse. Particularly inappropriate is the rustic porch. The words 'FIRE STATION' (which underneath have a finger pointing to the right) on the lamp outside, probably indicate that fire-fighting equipment was stored in the pub yard.

67. *The Bell and Horns, no. 31 North Road.* This c1900 picture was taken towards the end of this pub's life. It was closed in 1925 after having had about twenty different landlords since 1902, a sure sign of unprofitability. The premises became a petrol station.

*68. The Fox and Crown, Highgate West Hill.* The courtyard of this old pub is still evident attached to the house at no. 40. The place relished its notoriety after the landlord saved the young Queen Victoria from serious injury in 1837, when he arrested her runaway coach on the steep hill. An enormous coat-of-arms is displayed on the building, and the chair in which the Queen recovered from the experience is placed in a prominent position by the front door. The building was demolished in 1895.

## SAVING THE QUEEN

The fortunes of the Fox and Crown at no. 40 Highgate West Hill changed dramatically in 1837, soon after the young Queen Victoria had been crowned. A newspaper report of the time describes the affair thus:

'On Thursday evening, as Her Majesty and the Duchess of Kent, with their attendants, were proceeding from Highgate to Kentish Town, in descending the hill, the carriage, not having a drag-chain, proceeded at a very rapid pace, and the horses became restive and plunged violently, and great anxiety prevailed for the safety of the Royal party. Fortunately, however, Mr Turner, landlord of The Fox, rendered the most prompt assistance by affixing a chain to the wheel of the carriage. Her Majesty, who alighted at Mr Turner's house for a short time, while the preparations were being completed, was pleased to notice Mrs Turner and her children in the kindest manner, thanked Mr Turner for his prompt attention, and, seeing the ostler liberally remunerated for his trouble, took her departure for Kensington Palace, highly gratified at her providential escape.'

Lloyd, in his *History of Highgate* asserts that henceforth the pub was called the Fox and Crown to mark this event, but in fact that had been the full name of the place intermittently since it was first licensed early in the 18th century.

## HIGHGATE'S BREWERY

A substantial brewery existed on North Hill, on the site of the Hillcrest flats. Known as Park House in more recent years, it was obviously a brewery of some antiquity. It was certainly in business by 1670 and on an 1819 map of Hornsey, Highgate Wood, which was a continuation of the land attached to the brewery, was called Brewhouse Wood. In 1848 the house became a private lunatic asylum and seven years later a home for 'penitent prostitutes', an establishment which closed as late as 1940.

*69. (Facing top) The Gatehouse Tavern.* A photograph of *c*1885 before its 'Tudor' fascia.

*70. (Facing bottom) The Bull, North Hill.* From a drawing by J.T. Wilson, 1867.

*71. (Below) Park House, North Hill.* This engraving of the 1850s was made when the house was an Asylum for Idiots. The census of 1851 shows it containing 72 patients. Ten years later the census recorded 38 'penitents' instead, after a Penitentiary for prostitutes had been established here.

## MYSTERIOUS TUNNELS

The Gatehouse, of course, occupies a strategic place in the village. Here, the old toll road (North Road-North Hill) began, and the gatehouse originally was no more than a toll-collector's office with living accommodation; it seems to have developed into a tavern in the 17th century. Rumours of tunnels and secret compartments abound in Highgate. There are tales of a tunnel from The Spaniards to Kenwood, and from the Gatehouse to somewhere else. What *is* known is that in 1911, during renovation, two secret cupboards and a large chamber were found behind one of the chimneypieces at the Gatehouse. The Flask is another pub associated with tunnels, although it is never quite explained why (or how!) tunnels were built. More recently large tunnels or vaults were discovered on North Hill and these may have been associated with the brewery there.

72. A staircase still existing in 1907 in the gable of the Gatehouse Tavern, which previously led to the rooms over the gateway.

73. *The Flask Tavern, South Grove.* A drawing by A.R. Quinton, 1911.

## SWEARING ON THE HORNS

Highgate was renowned for a bizarre drinking custom called 'Swearing on the Horns': this is celebrated in numerous accounts and prints. The uninitiated were obliged to swear a nonsensical oath before a man holding aloft a pair of horns on a pole and it is fairly certain that the business resulted in more drink being bought than would otherwise have been the case. Sometimes whole coach parties arrived to take part in this commercial game, very like their modern counterparts who go to 'Elizabethan banquets' for indifferent food and childish rituals.

*74. Swearing at Highgate.*

"It's the custom at Highgate
that all who pass through,
Should be sworn on the horns
sir,  and so sir must you."

*75. Swearing on the Horns at Highgate.*

*76. Swearing on the Horns at the Gatehouse.* A postcard of the
beginning of this century.

# Various Recreations

## CRICKET

Cricketers from Highgate played at Westminster in 1790 and travelled to Woodford, Essex, in 1795. Shown here (*Illustration 77*) is the scoreboard of a match between a Highgate team and one from Kentish Town and Hampstead in 1794, for the enormous wager of 400 guineas. Highgate won easily and it is notable that their heroes on the day, Anderson and Sharp their opening batsmen, also took all the wickets with the exception of one.

## BOWLING GREENS

In 1661 the lord of Cantelowes manor granted a parcel of land between the Flask and Pond Square in trust to ten local residents. Their responsibility was the upkeep here of a bowling green for Highgate residents, which, according to the record, had existed since 'beyond the memory of man.' Unfortunately, the landlord of the Flask was given leave to dig it up in 1730 and it was never replaced. The Castle Inn, on the corner of Castle Yard and North Road, had a renowned bowling green which was used by local clubs and there was another behind the Red Lion by 1757.

*77. Scoreboard of a cricket match between teams from Highgate and Kentish Town and Hampstead, in 1794.*

On Monday the 2d of June, *1794* a grand match of cricket was played on Highgate Common, between eleven gentlemen of Highgate, and eleven gentlemen of **Kentish Town and Hampstead**, for four hundred guineas.

### HIGHGATE.

| FIRST INNINGS. | | SECOND INNINGS. | | |
|---|---|---|---|---|
| Anderson b Hack | 19 | b Hack | — | 1 |
| Sharp b Gable | 0 | c ditto | — | 16 |
| Hill b Shepperd | 12 | b ditto | — | 17 |
| Mr. Wheeler run out | 9 | b Gable | — | 27 |
| Parrott run out | 9 | b Shepperd | — | 5 |
| Melton b Shepperd | 2 | c Kentish | — | 0 |
| Batchellor b Hack | 7 | b Hack | — | 1 |
| French b Shepperd | 2 | hit wicket | — | 1 |
| Redwood c Hack | 4 | hit wicket | — | 28 |
| Cato c Kentish | 0 | not out | — | 1 |
| Spencer not out | 0 | hit wicket | — | 0 |
| Byes | 12 | Byes | | 20 |
| | 76 | | | 127 |

### KENTISH TOWN AND HAMPSTEAD.

| FIRST INNINGS. | | SECOND INNINGS. | | |
|---|---|---|---|---|
| Gable b Anderson | 5 | b Anderson | — | 8 |
| Kentish c Sharp | 0 | b Sharp | — | 3 |
| Knight run out | 2 | not out | — | 18 |
| Moor c Anderson | 0 | b Sharp | — | 1 |
| Hitchman c Spencer | 3 | b ditto | — | 3 |
| Shepperd b Sharp | 1 | stumpt ditto | — | 6 |
| Jones b ditto | 0 | b Anderson | — | 1 |
| Hack b Anderson | 1 | b ditto | — | 8 |
| Birch not out | 1 | b ditto | — | 1 |
| Wood b Sharp | 0 | stumpt Sharp | — | 4 |
| Randall b ditto | 0 | b Anderson | — | 0 |
| Byes | 1 | Byes | | 6 |
| | 14 | | | 59 |

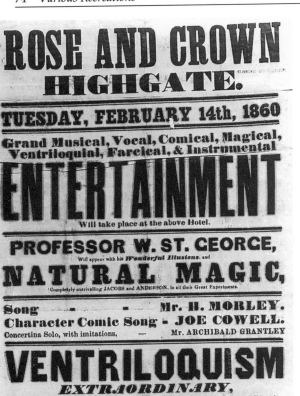

## THEATRICALS

Attached to the Castle Inn in Castle Yard in 1812 was Highgate's only theatre until recent times. Called The Larne, it was described as a converted barn or wheelwright's shop, fitted with pit, stalls and gallery. It had a short life.

More basic fare was provided in the pubs and the Rose and Crown handbill shown in *Illustration 78* reflects the Victorian fascination for magic, ventriloquists and music from far-off lands.

78. *An Entertainment at the Rose and Crown, 1860.*

79. A ticket for a Highgate Assembly, an evening of wining, dining and entertainment. The most usual venues were the White Lion in the High Street and the Gatehouse.

*80. The Castle, North Road.* The Castle, depicted in this *c*1906 postcard, stood on Highgate School land on the south-west corner of Castle Yard. It features quite a lot in the social life of the village, having once had the principal bowling green, the only theatre, and it was also the venue for a working men's club. Closed about 1872, it was then converted into a coffee and dining place, but demolished in 1928.

*81. The Ponds, Parliament Hill.* Rarely now do boys sail *quiet* model yachts on the ponds. Instead this pond is quite often used by men anxious to impress us with the speed and noise of their model speedboats, to the dismay of all ducks and most users of Parliament Hill. The Highgate Model Yacht Club was formed in 1850 with a well-filled rule book, and run by suitably named officers such as a Commodore.

82. *View from the Ponds at Highgate Hill.* In fact this 1822 view by T.M. Baynes depicts what is now the men's bathing pond by Millfield Lane. The ornate house of the comedian, Charles Mathews the elder (1776–1835), is in the background. At that time, as now, fishing was popular here.

83. *Croquet on the grounds of Highgate School.*

## PLAYING SOLDIERS

When England was threatened with invasion in 1803 volunteer defence corps were formed throughout the land. Highgate fielded a battalion of three hundred men called the Loyal Highgate Volunteers, which was supported by the leading residents. The major commandant was Nathaniel Harden of Winchester Hall (on Highgate Hill), and his officers included Addison of Highgate Brewery, James Ensor of Englefield House in the High Street, and John Prickett the local surveyor. Invasion threats subsided and the corps was disbanded in 1813.

Renewed worries occurred in 1859 and volunteer brigades were re-formed. In Highgate, Josiah Wilkinson, who lived in Fitzroy Park, was colonel of the Highgate Volunteer Rifles which eventually became two companies with headquarters at the newly-built Northfield Hall. This building in North Road was basically a drill hall but the Volunteers vainly hoped that it would become *the* hall for Highgate, accommodating all local groups including the Institution.

PRIVATE WITH GREAT COAT. OFFICER FULL DRESS. PRIVATE FULL DRESS. OFFICER UNDRESS.

S.W. SILVER & C?
CORNHILL.

*84. Highgate Volunteer Rifles.* The drawing, *c*1860, shows a private and an officer in formal and informal uniform.

85. *The North London Harriers, Highgate*. Running over Parliament Hill and the Heath was a well-established sport by the end of the last century. The famous Highgate Harriers were formed in 1879 from two cricket teams attached to the Magdala pub in Hampstead.

# Highgate Cemetery

## THE CROWDED CHURCHYARDS

At the beginning of the 19th century the state of London churchyards was a disgrace. Parishes found that despite enlargements or the acquisition of burial grounds far away from the parish church, they still could not cope with the demand for burial space. Quite unsavoury practices occurred, such as the exhumation of old remains so that new ones might take their place, or the burying of corpses much closer to the surface than was safe. Envious eyes were cast to the famous Père Lachaise cemetery in Paris, which showed how things could be done.

London was slow off the mark in having cemeteries, a result, probably, of the fragmented nature of the capital's government. Private companies, rather than local authorities, satisfied this need at first. These private graveyards with their distinctly ornamental grounds, a world away from the disorganised, malodorous churchyards, almost certainly helped to make burial a social event. More attention was given to the attendant marks of status in the size and decoration of the tombstone, the surroundings and position in the cemetery, the nature of the assembly, and in the quality of the funeral procession.

## HIGHGATE OPENED

The London Cemetery Company opened the old part of Highgate Cemetery in Swains Lane in 1839. The original architect was the maverick Stephen Geary, whose main claim to fame was the design of the first gin palace in London and the King's Cross memorial which, despite its ugliness and short life, left a new place name in London. He was assisted by James Bunning who went on to design the Coal Exchange and the old Billingsgate Fish Market. Both architects are buried here.

Highgate residents did not welcome this 'great garden of sleep' on the grounds of the old Ashurst House. But once its meandering paths, decorated

*86. Highgate Cemetery and St Michael's Church.* This postcard of *c*1906 shows the terrace at the top end of the old cemetery, beneath the church of St Michael. To the left is the mausoleum of the Beer family. Julius Beer, a financier from Frankfurt, was also proprietor of *The Observer* newspaper from 1870 to 1880.

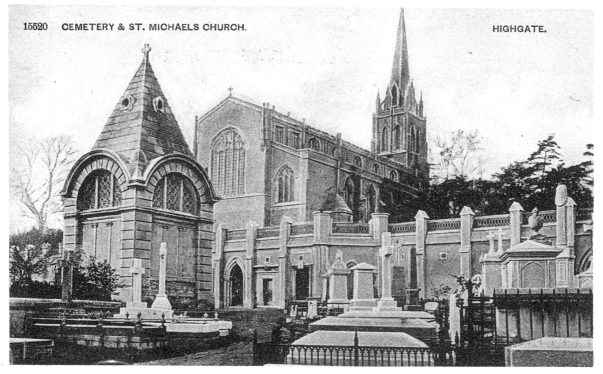

15520   CEMETERY & ST. MICHAELS CHURCH.                                           HIGHGATE.

*87. Plan for Highgate Cemetery.* **This design was produced by Stephen Geary, the cemetery company's architect. He planned a non-conformist chapel towards the centre of the cemetery together with a tunnel leading down to the forecourt for the transportation of the coffins. There was no provision for a Church of England chapel – presumably the intention was to use the church of St Michael instead. To the bottom left are catacombs, subsequently located at the top of the cemetery.**

PANORAMIC PICTURE OF THE FUNERAL OF TOM SAYERS.

*88. The funeral procession of Tom Sayers as it passed Holly Village, 1865.* Funerals could be vast affairs for popularly acclaimed people. Sayers was one of the last of the bare-fisted pugilists beloved of the English. In 1860 he fought 37 rounds against an American fighter before the contest was declared a draw.

with flowers and shrubs, had been seen they applied for keys so that they could walk there whenever they pleased.

The original Cemetery is, of course, on a spectacular site. High up on the terrace at the rear of St Michael's there is a wonderful view of London. Beneath it are the spooky catacombs, and further down, by the gates, the chapel building with its tunnel beneath Swains Lane for the transfer of coffins to the lower cemetery.

In common with its contemporaries such as Kensal Green, Norwood and Nunhead, Highgate Cemetery was a spectacular success, so much so that the lower ground was opened in 1856.

## RESTING PLACE OF THE FAMOUS

A large number of notable people are buried here. They include George Eliot, Radclyffe Hall, Herbert Spencer, Michael Faraday and Sir Rowland Hill. In the lower cemetery Karl Marx is now interred and his grave, marked by an extraordinary bust, is visited by sympathisers and the curious throughout the year. The funeral of the pugilist, Tom Sayers, in 1865 attracted thousands and was sufficiently notable to be represented in print (*Illustration 88*). The funeral in 1888 of James Selby, a famous coachman, included a procession a mile long; at the time of his burial the omnibus and cab drivers of the west end of London appeared with crape bows on their whips in memory of someone who had set the speed record for London to Brighton and back, and who was so devoted to his work that to remove his hat from his head in very cold weather it was necessary to pour on hot water.

Considerable public interest centred on the Cemetery in 1907 in connection with the grave of the furniture dealer, Thomas Charles Druce, who had been buried here in 1864. It was claimed that Druce had been, in fact, the wealthy 5th Duke of Portland and that the Duke lived a double life, one as a furniture seller and another as a reclusive aristocrat. On this premise the widow of Druce's son claimed some of the Duke's estate when he died in 1896 and this claim was carried on by *her* son when she had been removed to a lunatic asylum. The claimants insisted that 'Druce' had not died in 1864 and that his funeral was a sham, with the coffin being filled with lead or stones. This unlikely tale was put to the test in December 1907 when a long-awaited and well-guarded exhumation took place at Highgate, but the hopes of

## THE OPENING OF THE DRUCE COFFIN.

Excitement at the cemetery gates.

A strong force of police within and without the gates to warn off intruders

YESTERDAY'S SCENES OUTSIDE HIGHGATE CEMETERY. (Graphic Photo Union.)

*89. The Opening of the Druce Coffin.* This event attracted a great deal of macabre interest and invoked a strong police guard.

*90. Highgate Cemetery*. An engraving of the 1860s.

the Druces and the newspapers were dashed when human remains were found inside the coffin.

In recent years the Cemetery has fallen on hard times. The owners claimed that insufficient income had been put aside for its perpetual maintenance, and gradually it fell into neglect despite the devotion of its tiny staff. There were alarming rumours that it would be sold for re-development, although this was probably never a real possibility. But no-one wanted the job of maintaining it and it has only been through the energy and commitment of The Friends of Highgate Cemetery that it retains its attraction today.

# The Cable Tramway

A Scottish engineer, Andrew Smith Hallidie, invented the cable tramway in San Francisco which now so delights tourists. His assistant, William Eppelsheimer, turned his attention to London and came to Highgate, where the steep gradient almost precluded the use of horse-trams. He formed a limited company and was fortunate to receive the endorsement of Sir Sydney Waterlow of Fairseat in the High Street, who had seen the cable cars in America and did not seem to mind that they would clang past his house in Highgate.'The machinery is very simple', Waterlow claimed, 'rarely if ever out or order'. This was an optimistic assessment.

The tramway was opened in May 1884 and in the first seventeen days, over 50,000 passengers tried it. The route was from the Archway Tavern, then the terminus for a number of tram lines, and Highgate Village. The cars were connected to an endless cable powered by an engine-house in the High Street, and at each terminus the cars were revolved on a turntable so as to face the reverse direction.

The tramway's popularity was assured by the opening of Waterlow Park in 1891 but it was then that its troubles mounted. It was dogged by accidents and poor maintenance and once, when an influential local dignitary was on board, the brakes failed. It was closed for five years and when it reopened there was more trouble when, in 1899, a car full of passengers went out of control; it was found that both driver and conductor were drunk. More loss of revenue occurred when an electrified tram route began operating along Archway Road and then, in 1908, the London County Council bought it up cheaply so that it could be electrified. As part of the improvements, the track was made double all the way along and, ironically, one wing of Waterlow's house had to be demolished to make room.

The last cable cars were seen off in style in 1909. The employees had a farewell dinner and 'popular airs led by a man playing a cornet were also sung, each car as it went off the service being greeted by singing *Auld Lang Syne*. The climax was reached when the last car started on its journey down the hill. People fought to get on. Everyone seemed to possess coloured lights, crackers, fireworks and sticks. The conductor made a brave attempt to collect fares, but so great was the crush that he was unable to get beyond the top of the staircase.' The English male's love-affair with antiquated transport is not new.

*91. Building the track for the Highgate Cable Tramway.* **This photograph of** *c*1883 **is taken just below the Old Crown on Highgate Hill.**

92. *Advertisement for the Cable Tramway – the first in Europe*. Once again, the view is just below the Old Crown.

93. *The opening of the Cable Tramway in May 1884..*

94. *A Cable Tramway car.* A Highgate Schoolboy stands by the side.

HIGHGATE. A Cable Tramcar.

95. An electric tram in the village outside Attkins the pork butchers.

96. Children watching the moving cable beneath the track. Note the wonderful emptiness of the road. Crown Cottages, which are shown south of the Old Crown, are now demolished and replaced by a car park.

*97. Archway Tavern in the 1870s.* For various reasons this pub became the terminus for a number of transport routes – it still is. Here, bus drivers and transport workers of all kinds, including the horses, fed and drank.

*98. The Woodman, Archway Road.* This postcard of *c*1906 shows an electric tram.

*99. Trolleybuses in Highgate Village.* This scene will be remembered by many Highgate residents. The photograph was taken in June 1960.

*100. Highgate Station.* The railway from Finsbury Park to East Finchley via Highgate was opened in 1867 under the aegis of the Great Northern Railway. In 1873 a spur to this line was built skirting Highgate Wood to go under Muswell Hill Road up to Alexandra Palace. Its profitability depended entirely on that of the Palace.

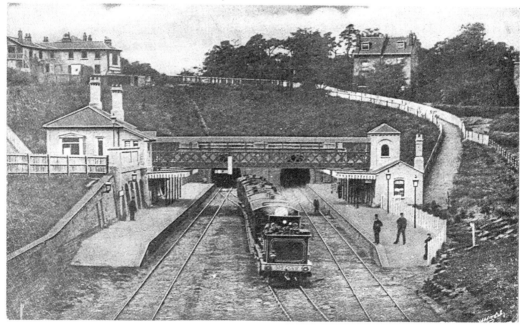

# More Grand Houses

## THE SOUTHAMPTON ESTATE

Some of the classiest villas in Highgate were built *c*1840 on the Southampton Estate. Fitzroy House, as we have seen (*page 36*) had had a remarkably short life, having been demolished by 1826. In its place Beechwood, in Hampstead Lane, was built in 1839 for the barrister Nathaniel Basevi, and designed by his brother the talented architect, George Basevi, whose career was tragically cut short by a fall from the roof of Ely Cathedral. The Basevis were a distinguished Anglo-Jewish family – an aunt was Disraeli's mother – but the brothers were both converted Christians and George was able to send his five sons to Highgate School because of this. Nathaniel mar-ried the niece of Sir Robert Peel – the politician visited here often. Subsequent residents included Edward Perronet Sells, a coal merchant who sold out to Charrington's, and Oswald Lewis, son of John Lewis the store owner.

George Basevi lived at The Elms in Fitzroy Park, which he designed himself in 1839. Holly Court (later an LCC school), in Merton Lane, was built the same year.

Very large houses were built in 1839 on the Highgate West Hill fringe of the Estate, mainly occupied by successful business men or lawyers. These included the group which still exists at the foot of the hill (up to no. 14) and those which have been taken over by the Russian Trade Delegation. A start was made the same year on Millfield Place, where three substantial villas, with views across the ponds, were built.

*101. Sale Plan of the Southampton Lodge Estate, 1908.* Southampton Lodge was one of the principal houses of Highgate. It was built in 1845 and from 1849 until 1903 it was occupied by Josiah Wilkinson, solicitor, whose public career included a long membership of the Metropolitan Board of Works and a persistent interest in the volunteer rifles movement.

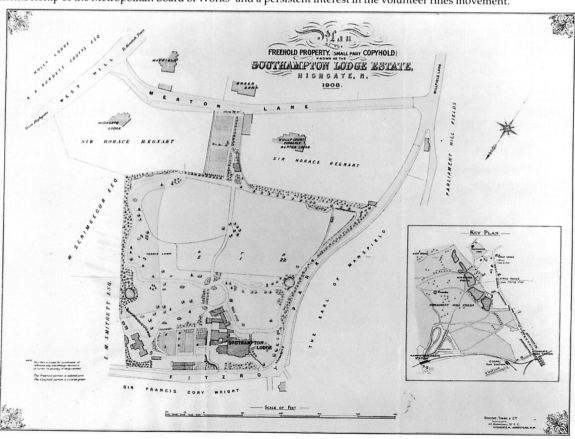

The Southampton Estate in Highgate was put up for sale in 1840; the prospectus shows the land divided for the erection of numerous, but spacious, villas, but the building invasion didn't, in fact, happen. Only five mansions of any size were built on the ample acres during the rest of the century. Southampton Lodge was one of them, home from 1845, when it was built, until 1903 of the Volunteer Rifles' commander, Josiah Wilkinson; he was for a long time a member of the Metropolitan Board of Works. The house is now gone, as are the other four.

The largest house was yet to come. Caen Wood Towers (more recently called Athlone House) was built by Salomons and Jones in *c*1871. Generally, it was owned by prosperous businessmen, such as Francis Reckitt (of dye fame) and Sir Cory Francis-Wright, an enormously rich coal merchant.

*102. Caen Wood Towers.* This vast pile, more lately known as Athlone House, superseded another well-known house – Dufferin Lodge, the home of the 1st Earl of Dufferin, prominent politician and diplomat in the 19th century.

103. *View in Mr Bodkin's grounds at Highgate*. Painting by W. Dickes. William Henry Bodkin, an Assistant Judge, lived at no. 34 Highgate West Hill from 1851 to 1876. His son, William Peter, chairman of various public utilities and the Westminster Fire Office, followed him here. The house, West Hill Place, was taken over by the St Pelegia's Home in 1920. An earlier resident here was Thomas Ridgway, the tea merchant.

104. *The Eagles, West Hill, Highgate*. This house, no. 33 Highgate West Hill, became part of the Russian Trade Delegation complex. Before the last war it was the home of a prominent Conservative politician.

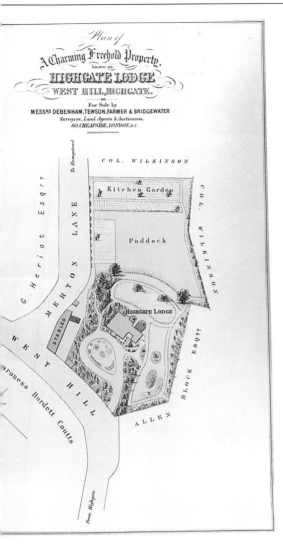

*105. Plan of Highgate Lodge.* This sale plan is *c*1903. The house's most prominent resident was Sir Horace Regnart, vice-chairman of Maple's, the furniture company, and Alderman of St Pancras, in which capacity he had a leading role in the development of St Pancras Almshouses in Kentish Town.

*106. Thomas Coutts (1735–1822).* Coutts, together with his brother, founded the Coutts banking house in the Strand which then, as today, was banker to the royal family. He married, first, the servant of his brother; by her he had three daughters, all of whom married well – the third to the politician Sir Francis Burdett. Soon after his wife died Coutts married his mistress of long-standing, the actress Harriot Mellon, to whom he bequeathed his vast fortune, which in turn was left to Burdett's daughter, Angela.

## HOLLY LODGE

On the other side of Highgate West Hill a fairly modest detached summer villa was built in 1807, which in 1809 was let to the actress Harriot Mellon, the mistress of the fabulously rich Scottish banker, Thomas Coutts. On his wife's death, Coutts married her and after his she remarried, this time to the Duke of St Albans, descendant of the baby dangled out of Lauderdale House in the 17th century (*page 20*). In 1849, after the death of the Duke, the most famous occupant of Holly Lodge arrived, Angela Burdett-Coutts, who had inherited the bulk of the Coutts fortune. She was, with the exception of Queen Victoria, the richest woman in the country and she was to acquire an impressive reputation for philanthropy, although few of her ventures have survived to modern times.

Throughout her long residence here she gradually acquired land to the north and south, all the time protecting the borders of her estate and by the time the land went up for sale in the 1920s it was one of the largest open spaces in private hands in London.

Two local features are reminders of her. One is the landscaping and the rhododendrons in Holly Lodge Gardens and the other is Holly Village in Swains Lane which romantics persist in saying was built for her estate workers but which was, in reality,

tenanted by 'clerks and commercial travellers'.

Miss Coutts was made a Baroness in 1871 (the first in England in her own right) and ten years later, when she was 67, she shocked society and commoners alike by marrying a 30-year-old American.

The Estate was put up for sale in 1923 after his death and it was purchased by an Alderman Davis, whose plan was for a garden suburb for middle-class residents. This is substantially what transpired although it will be seen from his original plan (*Illustration 111*) that the Tudor-style blocks of flats for single lady workers were an afterthought.

107. *Angela Burdett-Coutts.*

108. *Holly Lodge.*

*109. Holly Village, Highgate, lately erected by Miss Burdett Coutts.* Holly Village was built in 1865 as a garden village by Henry Darbishire, an architect best known for his tenement blocks for working class people. A plaque now fixed to the ornate porchway asserts the commonly held belief that they were built for Coutts workers, but there is no evidence for this. A contemporary magazine said that the dwellings were 'suitable residences for clerks, commercial travellers and so on, the class of persons for whom they have been designed', and six years later the census return shows none of the residents to have connections, at least occupational, with Coutts. Holly Village was purchased by its tenants in 1921 for £5000.

*110. Holly Lodge Estate Sale Notice, 1907.* The houses north of Holly Lodge were part of the Estate from the beginning of the 19th century. This sale notice gives the rents of Holly Terrace at the time.

THE PREMISES.

# A DELIGHTFUL OLD FAMILY RESIDENCE

KNOWN AS

## "*South Grove House,*" No. 19, *South Grove,*

being a continuation of WEST HILL, and having

### Extensive Gardens and Grounds,

together with GREEN-HOUSES, STABLING, and PREMISES IN THE REAR, to which there is a Side Entrance to BROMWICH WALK.

# THE ADJOINING RESIDENCE,
## No. 18, SOUTH GROVE,

approached through a GARDEN FORECOURT, with Good Garden in the Rear, next St. Michael's Church.

*The foregoing House Property is Let to and in the occupation of Tenants of a superior class, as follows :—*

| PREMISES. | TENANT. | TENANCY. | RENT PER ANN. £ s. d. |
|---|---|---|---|
| 1, HOLLY TERRACE.... | Mrs. H. BARRS ........ | Yearly Midsummer ............................ | 100 0 0 |
| 2, HOLLY TERRACE.... | G. H. BURGIN ........ | Agreement which will expire at Michaelmas, 1908 ............................ | 52 10 0 |
| 3, HOLLY TERRACE.... | HERBERT RAND ........ | ,, ,, ,, | 82 0 0 |
| 4, HOLLY TERRACE.... | ARTHUR B. WEST .... | Lease which will expire at Lady-day, 1914............................ | 100 0 0 |
| (With this House is Let Garden Plot marked "A" on Plan, with power to the Lessor to resume Possession without compensation). | | | |
| 5, HOLLY TERRACE.... | F. J. FORMAN ............ | Agreement which will expire at Mid-summer, 1908............................ | 60 0 0 |
| 6, HOLLY TERRACE.... | F. S. DONNISON ........ | Yearly ............................................ | 75 0 0 |
| 7, HOLLY TERRACE.... | S. D. CRAY ................ | Agreement which will expire at Mid-summer, 1908............................ | 40 0 0 |
| 8, HOLLY TERRACE.... | FISHER WHITE ........ | ,, ,, ,, | 55 0 0 |
| 9, HOLLY TERRACE.... | H. V. HOOYDONK .... | ,, ,, ,, | 42 10 0 |
| 10, HOLLY TERRACE.... | Mrs. M. H. NICOL .... | ,, ,, ,, | 45 0 0 |
| (With this House is Let Garden Plot marked "B" on Plan, Rent Free, with power to the Lessor to resume Possession at any time by giving one week's notice). | | | |

Carried forward........ £652 0 0

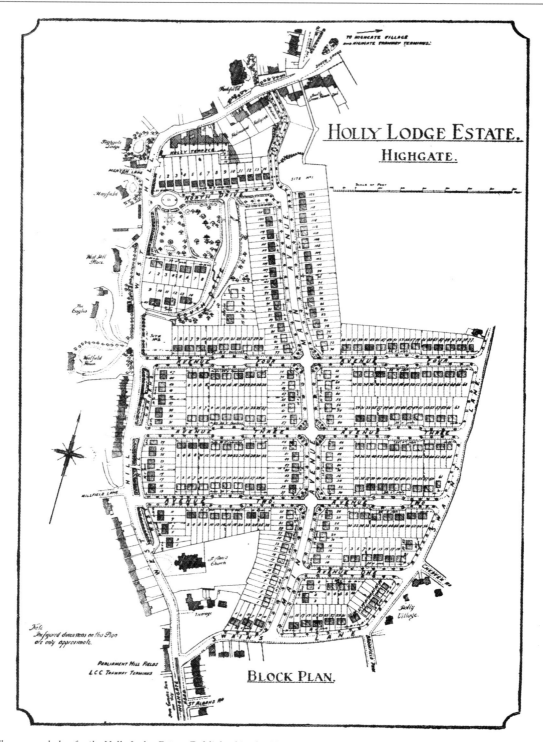

*111. The proposed plan for the Holly Lodge Estate.* Published in the *Hampstead and Highgate Express*, December 1923.

112. *(Top) The Estate, Highgate.* This postcard view shows the top of Hillway at its junction with Holly Lodge Gardens.

113. *(Left) Sale notice for the Parkfield Estate.* The Parkfield Estate, here being sold in 1889, consisted of the house now supplanted by Witanhurst, the Fox and Crown pub, and the frontage of land to Fitzroy Park which has recently been developed.

114. *(Right) West Hill Lodge.* No. 37 Highgate West Hill had been the home of William and Mary Howitt from 1857 to 1868; Florence Nightingale also used it after returning from the Crimean War. The house was demolished and rebuilt in 1927.

# A Place for Schools

## BIG HOUSES TRANSFORMED

Before Highgate School became respected and admired, the large houses of Highgate accommodated numerous private schools to which the wealthier local families sent their children.

There was a school as early as 1710 in part of the Old Hall and by the end of that century Misses Kearton and Sheldon ran a girls' boarding establishment at Lauderdale House, Ann Teulon had a school in Winchester House opposite and there was a small boys' school in Englefield House in the High Street. Nearby was Holly House Academy on the site of Holly Terrace. These were just some of the many where ill-paid clergymen and unmarried women augmented their incomes, and their numbers multiplied in the 19th century.

## GROVE HOUSE SCHOOL FOR BOYS

One of the better-known private schools was Grove House at no. 46 Highgate West Hill. It was founded, probably in the 1830s, for both boys and girls. An advertisement of the time said 'Young ladies are liberally boarded and carefully instructed in every department of plain and ornamental education.' Alfred Dickinson took over as head of the boys' school in 1885; the schoolroom in the adjacent building took three classes without any dividing walls. The art master of the time was Francis Barraud, the designer of the *His Master's Voice* trademark of the dog and gramophone.

115. *Grove House School.* No. 46 Highgate West Hill. The main house was used for boarding and the annexe took three classes without any dividing walls. The school closed in 1930.

# CHANNING SCHOOL

Channing School for Girls was begun in 1885 by the Misses Matilda and Emily Sharpe, with the assistance of the Rev. Robert Spears. They were all Unitarians and the school was for members of that religion, which had a strong tradition of educating their daughters: Harriet Martineau and Mrs Gaskell were products of that custom. Miss Matilda, an eccentric, resourceful and highly prudish woman, was the driving force. Gentlemen who came to lecture were chaperoned wherever they went, and this presumably applied to the 22-year-old Marconi when he visited the school in 1897 to demonstrate his discovery of wireless telegraphy.

The school was housed in Sutherland House, a large double-fronted building on the corner of The Bank and Cholmeley Park, the latter then a lane which led to the mansion Cholmeley Lodge. In the 1920s the adjoining houses in the terrace were absorbed, but this still wasn't enough. In 1926 Fairseat across the road, on the site of Sir Roger Cholmeley's house, and more recently the home of Sir Sydney Waterlow, was taken on.

116. *Channing House High School*. The original school building of 1888 was Sutherland House (shown here), at the corner of Highgate Hill and Cholmeley Park.

117. In the gardens of Channing House School.

## TEACHING THE POOR

After 1829 it became difficult for poorer local residents to have their children educated at Highgate School, and so in 1833 a National School was erected next to the almshouses for this purpose, and an Infant School followed six years later in Castle Yard.

These were far from satisfactory. The educational provision was very elementary and parents tended to take their children away from them and put them to employment as early as possible. Highgate was fortunate in that one of its most prominent residents, Harry Chester *(see page 45)*, was a highly-placed and influential educational reformer. What he proposed in the Village as a private resident and what he secured through his professional clout, was a National School which enshrined the latest principles of education – of teaching through manual skills and of learning through contact with Nature. A substantial building, St Michael's Schools in North Road, was erected, with quite lavish grounds attached. Also, a fashionable architect, Anthony Salvin, was engaged in this showpiece establishment. Four acres were transformed into a model farm and scholars were encouraged not only to work in it but to manage it, as training for the outside world. Girls were given a much more thorough grounding in house management than was to be found elsewhere.

Unfortunately, but inevitably, the value of learning agricultural skills diminished as parents realised that what the world wanted was more clerks than cowhands, and gradually the school became a conventional elementary school.

118. *College House School, Highgate Hill, 1870.* This stood to the south of the Old Crown public house and is seen also in Illustration 46. Charging 25 guineas per annum, it had an educational system 'peculiarly calculated to excite a spirit of emulation among the pupils . . .

119. *St Michael's National School, 1851.*

# Surrounded by Open Spaces

## FIGHTING ON ALL FRONTS

Highgate is blessed with open spaces of considerable variety. In walking distance are the panoramas of Parliament Hill and the picturesque ponds, cultivated Kenwood, the woods near Highgate Station and the gardens of Waterlow Park. Little of this greenery was easily acquired.

The battle to save Hampstead Heath from development had been won in 1871 after a very long, articulately led, campaign. In the final years of sparring with the Hampstead lord of the manor the residents had had the backing of the newly-formed Commons Preservation Society. By the time of victory even the House of Commons had begun to believe that human beings needed green lungs in their cities, and the remaining commons and heaths, gained some protection.

The trouble at Highgate was that the open spaces were private property. Parliament Hill, for example, belonged to Lord Mansfield and there were no legal restrictions on its sale and development. Highgate Wood and Queen's Wood (or Gravel Pit Wood and Churchyard Bottom as they were then called) both belonged to the Bishop of London. Fortunately, Mansfield was a rich man, in no urgent need to capitalise on the lands which gave him the best view in London, and the Bishop of London had ample acres of quite uncomplicated landscape still to develop.

*120. The tumulus on Parliament Hill Fields.* This mound has excited the interest of antiquarians and archaeologists for a long time. This drawing by Dr William Stukeley an enthusiastic if occasionally misguided antiquarian, was made in 1725. It was probably he that began the legend that the tumulus marks the grave of Queen Boudicca. On the assumption that it contained some sort of burial the mound was excavated in 1894, but, sadly, nothing of importance was found.

*Immanuentii tumulus.*

*1.1. May 1725*

## HIGHGATE WOOD

In the campaign to save Highgate Wood the blunt question was: Who would put up the money? The local vestry, Hornsey, had very limited resources and powers; the area was outside London and the Metropolitan Board of Works had no remit, let alone appetite, to acquire land outside its own boundaries; there was, at the time, no county authority for Middlesex which could be appealed to.

The odd solution was to persuade the City of London to buy it for the use of its own residents – there was now a frequent train service to Highgate. In 1886 the City bought Highgate Wood and still administer it today. Whether any of its residents use (or even know) the wood is unknown, but we must be grateful to their hard-headed predecessors for their gesture.

## PARLIAMENT HILL BOUGHT

The campaign to save Parliament Hill had been going on for some years. It had been complicated by the need to buy also a swathe of land called the East Park Estate in Hampstead (by today's Hampstead Ponds) which had, for years, been the proposed site of the lord of the manor's building development. This, too, was private land and, in theory, the current lord of the manor was free to build on it. In doing so he would have seriously depleted the value of Parliament Hill as an open space. So, both open spaces had to be bought at the same time and negotiations did not run smoothly. But in the end, with contributions from the appropriate authorities, the day was won in 1889.

*121. Garden party on Parliament Hill, 1885.* To raise money for the acquisition of the Fields the organisers arranged many social events including a garden party.

## AN UNEXPECTED GIFT

The next open space came without campaigns or expense. Sir Sydney Waterlow, printer and former Lord Mayor of London, gave his estate at Highgate, which included Lauderdale House and the grounds which now form Waterlow Park, to the London County Council. He was an enormously rich man, as befitted a man who printed banknotes. He had twelve children and in the year of his mayoralty his house, Fairseat, contained 17 servants. He was never able to secure the freehold of Fairseat and neither was the LCC after him, so that the house could be incorporated into the park. In the end, this was probably fortunate because the possession of Fairseat (which, after all, still stands) would have probably meant the demolition of Lauderdale House as being superfluous.

## QUEEN'S WOOD

The saving of Queen's Wood may be rightly attributed to one man's enthusiasm. He was Henry Reader Williams, by all accounts a rather egocentric chairman of Hornsey Local Board, whose deeds are commemorated by the clock tower in Crouch End. He proposed that the local Vestry buy the land, so that it would become a charge on the rates. This idea caused considerable opposition in an era when the containment of the parish rate was almost a sacred duty and it was a long and acrimonious campaign that was waged. Victory was achieved in 1898, after Williams had died.

*122. Sir Sydney Waterlow (1822–1906).* Waterlow was head of the printing company of that name and Lord Mayor of London in 1873. His philanthropic career included the promotion of housing for the poorer classes.

*123. Waterlow Park.* From a postcard, 1908.

124. *Swains Lane, 1906.* By W. West. The artist, instead of signing his illustration, has put his name on a plate on the nearest cottage.

125. *The house of Dr Elisha Coysh, Swains Lane.* In 1659 Dr Coysh was licensed to lay three yards of pipes from a well just north of the gates of the present old Highgate Cemetery to his own house.

# Side Roads

### SWAINS LANE

This meandering road is one of the oldest in Highgate. It is mentioned in court rolls of the 15th century, occasionally spelt Swines Lane. Basically it was a service track between fields but it also marked from quite early times a division between two major estate holdings, one of those held by Sir Roger Cholmeley on the Waterlow Park side. The *c*1800 map of this area (*Illustration 27*) shows a row of cottages on the west side, approximately on the site of the entrance to the old Highgate Cemetery, for which they were demolished. One of those cottages was that occupied by Dr Elisha Coysh, celebrated during the Great Plague of 1665 as a physician who could effect cures.

At the top of the Lane in the 16th century, fronting South Grove, stood a large house of about twenty rooms. Thomas Throckmorton, who lived there in 1603, laments in a letter that year to Sir Robert Cecil: 'I have made my abode in Highgate the most part of this year for my urgent business about London. My house is infected with small pox. I was never more unable to travel from the aches that have fallen upon my limbs.'

### BROMWICH WALK

Branching off near what is now the foot of Hillway, and emerging in South Grove, was an old track which acquired the name of Bromwich Walk from Thomas Bromwich, whose residence, South Grove House, overlooked its upper entrance. The path was there well before Bromwich and it is even suggested that it predates Highgate West Hill as the main track north from Kentish Town. Whatever its age, it acquired status as a public right of way, which was alright when it went between fields, but when Thomas Coutts gradually bought up the land on both sides the last thing he wanted was people using it. He tried to close it, but there was public outcry, and instead he built a high wall on both sides as it went through his land and, enclosed in this way, it is hardly surprising that it obtained a rather dubious and unsavoury reputation as a scene of misdeeds. Baroness Coutts continued the closure attempts but was not successful until 1903 when she traded a piece of land to widen Swains Lane. The remains of the old route may be seen in the path which leads from Swains Lane to the garage at the rear.

## MILLFIELD LANE

The whereabouts of the mill which gave this pleasant road its name is not known. It is fairly clear that it was south of Kenwood, in the neighbourhood of Parliament Hill, but no trace survives on the maps or in the field names. The map reproduced in *Illustration 32* calls the road Milford Lane, indicating a road adjacent to a ford by a mill. If this is a correct naming then it would indicate that the mill was on the river Fleet, which runs through today's ponds, and that it was probably a water mill and not a windmill.

Millfield Cottage is a development from the house of the supervisor for the Hampstead Waterworks Company, who controlled the ponds. The West Hill Court flats are on the site of Ivy House, a whimsically decorated house occupied by Charles Mathews, a celebrated comedian of his time, in the 1820s.

The northern end of Millfield Lane goes up to Kenwood, though it is now a footpath only. It has been suggested that this was the original route up the hill and there are some grounds for thinking that it was. On this upper stretch stood the very old Fitzroy Farmhouse, which was mostly destroyed by fire in 1971, and has been handsomely rebuilt using many of the 16th century timbers.

*126. Ivy Cottage, Millfield Lane.* This cottage was occupied by Charles Mathews (1776–1835), a celebrated comedian committed enough to make jokes on his own deathbed. The house was substantially rebuilt in 1833 for James Shoolbred, owner of a large furnishing store in the Tottenham Court Road. West Hill Court flats are on the site.

Mr SHOOLBREDS VILLA ON THE RISE OF HIGHGATE HILL.

FOR SALE BY AUCTION BY Mr GEO. ROBINS AT THE AUCTION MART, ON THURSDAY, JULY 29th 1841.

## HOLLY TERRACE

In its way this is the oddest terrace in Highgate, since its front doors face a fairly hidden pathway and its back doors, or some of them, let on to the main road. This unusual plan probably deterred many people in the 19th century since it somehow lacked prestige, but it has many compensations nowadays. The row was built from 1807 on the site of the house and grounds of Holly House Academy, but for most of its existence it was part of the Coutts estate and was, in fact, sold as individual houses when that estate was disposed of at the beginning of this century.

## JACKSON'S LANE

This road derives its name from Joseph Jackson who lived at Hillside, the house with the overhanging bay window at the narrowest part, in the early 19th century. In effect, the road is a continuation of Shepherds Hill and most likely its dip down to Archway Road is artificial and due to the general levelling of land here when the toll road was being built.

*27. Jackson's Lane.* Postcard, *c*1906, looking towards Southwood Lane.

## TOWNSEND'S YARD

This alley, which runs down to the Highgate Garden Centre off the High Street, was named from the Townshend family, builders, who lived in the house on the corner of the yard shown in *Illustration 171*. By the 19th century Townsend's Yard contained many of the slums which existed in Highgate. Some of them are shown in *Illustration 129* – the ones on the left were not demolished until 1934. Jack Foster, the village water-carrier, had a cottage here which looked picturesque if not healthy. A writer in the 1940s said that this shack was still standing, decayed and ruinous and used by the market gardener as a store. According to the 1851 census Foster shared the cottage with his wife, son, two granddaughters and a female servant.

128. *Townsend's Yard*. Drawing by W. West, *c*1905.

129. *Timber cottages in Townsend's Yard prior to demolition.* Mr Kerry, the builder, is demonstrating how much out of **perpendicular these old cottages were in 1890.**

# FITZROY PARK

This lane is the former driveway to Fitzroy or South-ampton House, roughly on the site of today's Beech-wood. There was a flurry of development from *c*1839 when some of the principal houses, such as Beech-wood and The Elms were built. A house called Hill-side was built in 1846. Its first occupants, the Misses Gillies, were related to Dr Thomas Southwood Smith, the leading public health reformer, who often stayed here. The ladies received a visit from the storyteller Hans Christian Andersen once, but the young chil-dren there were acutely disappointed in the rather cold personality of the Dane. Charles Lee Lewes, stepson of George Eliot, was a later occupant – he was a member of the LCC and a leader in the fight to save Parliament Hill Fields.

Many people are curious about no. 10, a house built in 1934 by the architect Vincent Harris for him-self. It is rather charmless but it has a splendid site and lovely gardens, and it was left by him to Camden Council by way of thankyou for all the commissions that he had received from the old St Pancras Council.

130. *(Below) Merton Lane, looking towards the ponds.* From a postcard, *c*1906.

KENT'S YARD,
HIGHGATE, 1905.

W. WEST.

# Looking After the Poor

### SEEING THE DOCTOR

In the 18th century the favoured method for providing medical treatment for those who could hardly afford it was to set up Dispensaries. These establishments, overseen by a doctor, were subscribed by wealthier and charitable residents who could nominate non-paying patients to be treated. Highgate Dispensary was established in 1767 'for the relief of the poor of Highgate, Muswell Hill, Crouch End, Hornsey and Holloway'. The patients had to 'behave themselves decently and soberly' and were to 'conform strictly to such rules as are given them…or they will be immediately dismissed.' This venture, though not successful at first, lasted until 1911.

*31. (Facing page) Kent's Yard, 1905.* The last corndealer of ny note in the village was Marriott's at no. **58 High Street** his attractive weather-boarded shop is still there. **The** ard next to it, Kent's Yard, was named after a previous wner of the business. Cottages were at the end of this, as epicted here by W. West.

*32. Highgate Dispensary.* In 1880 the Dispensary moved ere, to no. 54 Highgate West Hill.

## ISOLATING THE ILL

Although it was usually impossible to cure people with serious diseases, especially if they had no money to pay for whatever treatment might exist, they could be isolated. People were sent away from the capital into buildings in the green fields and there incarcerated. One such place was the Leper Hospital on Highgate Hill, where the St Mary's wing of the Whittington Hospital now sprawls. This was established in 1473 but closed in the 17th century. Coincidentally the same site was chosen in 1846 for a Smallpox Hospital which had to be moved from the site of King's Cross Station when the Great Northern Railway built its terminus.

In 1869 the St Pancras Guardians of the Poor, trying to separate their infectious or ill paupers from the working ones, built an infirmary on Dartmouth Park Hill, but it was soon to be part of a general hospital system for the poorer classes. Other Poor Law infirmaries were built by Holborn on Archway Road (now the Archway wing) and Islington built their's next to the old Smallpox Hospital – St Mary is Islington's parish church and the present wing of the Whittington is named from that.

Thus all three wings of Whittington Hospital began life as poor infirmaries.

*133. The new Smallpox Hospital at Highgate.* This was built in 1846 after the site of its original building had been taken by King's Cross Station.

*134. St Pancras Infirmary, Highgate.* This building, opened in 1869, is now the Highgate Wing of Whittington Hospital. It was originally the Infirmary for poor people of St Pancras parish.

*135. Holborn Infirmary, Archway Road.* From a postcard of *c*1906. This building is now the Archway Wing of Whittington Hospital.

# HIGHGATE WORKING MEN'S CLUB.

## Summer Engagements, 1873.

THE MEMBERS ARE INVITED, DURING THE SEASON, TO SPEND AN EVENING IN THE GROUNDS OF THE PRESIDENT, COL. JEAKES (BUT THE DATE CANNOT AT PRESENT BE DEFINITELY FIXED); ALSO TO SPEND AN EVENING IN THE GROUNDS OF H. R. WILLIAMS, ESQ., OAK LODGE. THE DATES WILL BE POSTED IN THE CLUB AT LEAST A WEEK PRIOR TO EACH VISIT.

**MONDAY, August 4th, The ATHLETIC SPORTS,** in the Cholmeley Cricket Field, at 3 o'Clock.

(OF WHICH SPECIAL PROGRAMMES WILL BE ISSUED.)

**SEPTEMBER, On some convenient day, to be arranged later, the Club hope to visit the new City Library and Guildhall.**

WITH THE VIEW OF SUGGESTING INTERESTING AND INSTRUCTIVE RECREATION FOR THE SUMMER MONTHS, PRIZES HAVE BEEN KINDLY OFFERED AS FOLLOWS:—

## ESSAYS.

1. The use of Birds to the Gardener and Agriculturist, and the necessity for their Preservation.
   PRIZE, THE PRESIDENT  .  .  .  . £5.

2. The Dignity of Labour, and the proper Limit of Recreation.
   PRIZE, REV. J. VINEY  .  .  . £3.

## NATURAL HISTORY COLLECTIONS.

1. For the best Collection of named Ferns, Mosses, Grasses, and Wild Flowers.
   PRIZE, W. PIPER, ESQ.  .  .  .  .  .  .  . £2 10s.

2. For the best Collection of named Butterflies and Moths,
   FIRST PRIZE, H. R. WILLIAMS, ESQ.  .  .  .  . £2 10s.
   SECOND PRIZE, THE HON. SEC.  .  .  .  .  . £1 10s.

3. For the best named Collection of Insects (Land or Water.)
   PRIZE, ROBERT WATSON, ESQ.  .  .  .  .  . £2 10s.

### CONDITIONS OF COMPETITION FOR ABOVE.

ESSAYS.—That there shall not be less than three Competitors for each Essay, who must be Members of the Club of not less than three month's standing. Such Essay shall consist of at least 300 lines of original matter, to be plainly written on faint ruled foolscap paper. That the Essay shall be delivered to the Hon. Sec. in a sealed Envelope, not signed with Name of writer, but simply a motto written outside the Envelope, accompanied with a second sealed Envelope bearing the same motto, in which shall be written the Name and Address of the writer. That the Judges be E. T. Griffiths, Esq., Mr. Fawley, of the "North Middlesex Chronicle," and Mr. Hayns, of the "Hampstead and Highgate Express."

NATURAL HISTORY COLLECTIONS.—That there shall not be less than three Competitors for each Collection. That such Collections shall be made entirely by the Competing Members, collected within 10 miles of Highgate, and bear the common and scientific names (as far as possible), together with name of particular place where found. The Collections to be delivered at the house of Hon. Sec, by 20th Oct. next.
The Ferns, Mosses, and Wild Plants, may be either living or dried, or part of each, if properly displayed for Exhibition.
Judges : Butterflies, &c., The President, Professor Tomlinson, & Rev. W. D. Bodkin.
   ,,     For Plants, &c., Messrs. Cossard, Willard, and Winter.

The successful Essays will be read, the Collections Exhibited, and the Prizes publicly Presented, at the commencement of the Winter Course of Lectures.

J. H. LLOYD, Hon. Sec.

# RECREATION FOR THE WORKING MAN

It is to the credit of the Highgate worthies that they recognised that those who had no land should be provided with some so that they could grow their own produce. In 1847 six acres were purchased, (now part of the Highgate School playing fields) to let out to 184 Highgate residents. The allotment holders included six shoemakers, nineteen farmhands, a washerwoman, a bus driver, a deaf mute and a lunatic's attendant. Some people suggested that the scheme would render the poor unfit for ordinary work, and others objected that the gardeners might sit drinking and smoking there.

It was a successful scheme, in keeping with the strong horticultural tradition in Highgate (the Highgate Horticultural Society was formed in 1859 and still flourishes), but the School needed the lands in 1898.

The Congregational Church in South Grove was the first to form a Working Men's Association, in 1861, and the established church, St Michael's, retaliated with their Working Men's Institute the following year, but in 1872 the two groups merged and took up residence in Castle Yard, where John Lloyd, later to be secretary of the Institution, was the secretary. It would be interesting to find extant the essays submitted on 'The Dignity of Labour, and the proper Limit of Recreation' mentioned in *Illustration 136*!

# THE HOUSING PROBLEM

Highgate had few slums – it was, compared with some, a prosperous town, with many of its inhabitants employed in the large houses in the locality. But there were hovels. The most famous picture (*Illustration 129*) shows some houses in Townsend's Yard which were both unsanitary and unsafe. Off North Road stood York Buildings, a row of cottages built in 1815, only one of which had its own lavatory. The energetic Congregational minister, the Rev Josiah Viney, erected the Verandah Place dwellings in North Hill. It was declared that 'Each sitting room is papered and furnished with a cupboard, firerange and bake oven. The kitchen is furnished with grate, washing copper, sink, dusthole, coal box and shelves. The rents are 4/–d to 5/3d per week.' Viney's example was copied in 1865 when local people founded the Highgate Dwellings Improvement Company which built Coleridge Buildings on Archway Road.

*136. (Facing page) Highgate Working Men's Club. Summer Engagements, 1873.* The Club was formed from a merger of two church working men's organisations. It met at the old Castle Inn.

*137. (Below) York Buildings, North Road.* This 1911 photograph shows the range of about 20 cottages erected in 1815 by a local bricklayer. Only one had its own lavatory.

# Highgate at Prayer

church of St Michael's, opened in 1832 and designed by Lewis Vulliamy, is situated on higher ground than any other in London and its entrance is level with the cross on the top of St Paul's Cathedral.

## REPLACEMENT OF THE CHAPEL

As has been seen in the section on Highgate School, the old chapel attached to the School, which was habitually used by local residents, was eventually too small for their needs. An application to rebuild it was refused on the basis that the charity which owned the chapel and school was there to spend money on behalf of the charity, and not on the residents of Highgate. In the event, it was a fortuitous decision, because the population of the village grew at such a rate that an enlarged School chapel would have quickly become inadequate again.

The Ecclesiastical Commissioners were obliged to co-operate in building a new parish church for Highgate and a site was found by demolishing the old Ashurst House. The new building had the same long driveway that Ashurst had built, and at the rear, quite remarkable views over London. The new

*138. St Michael's Church.* A postcard of 1906.

*139. The Baptist Chapel in Southwood Lane.*

## DISSENT IN THE VILLAGE

Both Highgate and Hampstead were beyond the five mile limit within which non-conformist preachers could not operate. A Presbyterian meeting house was in Southwood Lane, on the site of the old Baptist Chapel, in the 1660s; John Storer, who lived in a cottage on the site of Church House, was preacher here in 1672. Rochemont Barbauld, husband of the writer Anna Barbauld, was a minister of this Presbyterian chapel, and so was the Rev. David Williams, the founder of the Royal Literary Fund.

The congregation of Presbyterians divided and a rival meeting house was set up across the road between the almshouses and Castle Yard. The original group sold their building to the Baptists in c1809. This latter congregation had originated in a mission from a church in Eagle Street, High Holborn. They appear to have rebuilt the old meeting house in c1836, and this is the building, with alterations, which Highgate School owns today.

Hardly any Catholics were registered in Highgate in the 17th century and there was no place of worship until 1858 when the Passionist Fathers bought the dilapidated former pub, the Black Dog, just behind today's St Joseph's church. Catholics were still not welcome and the founding fathers had to inspect the old property in disguise. In the latter part of the 19th century the number of Catholics increased considerably, mainly immigrant Irish working on railways and building sites. St Joseph's, designed by Albert Vicars, was opened in 1889.

The Congregational Church, originally a small affair in Southwood Lane, opened a new building in South Grove in 1859. This still survives but is now

W.WEST.

ST JOSEPH'S RETREAT,
HIGHGATE 1870.

Nº 10.

140. *St Joseph's Retreat, 1870.*

141. *The Congregational Church, South Grove.* This photograph was taken soon after the church opened in 1859.

used by the United Reformed Church, who themselves moved from the old Presbyterian church at the corner with Hornsey Lane.

Defoe found that Highgate was a favourite retreat of wealthy Jews. He was almost certainly referring to the Mendes da Costa family who lived in Cromwell House (when they possessed the house in 1675 they were the first Jews in England to own property since the Middle Ages). A private synagogue was installed in the house.

# The Highgate Ponds

## WATER FOR LONDON

Quite the most spectacular introduction to Highgate is a diversion off Highgate West Hill into Millfield Lane. Along here are some of the beautiful ponds – the benches around them provide some of the most peaceful vantage points in London except when the irritating roar of model speed boats cuts through the air. Legend has it that these stretches of water were cut by monks, but their history is more prosaic than that and more interesting.

By the end of the 16th century the City of London was short of water. It had permission to utilise springs outside its borders and in 1589 it attempted to marshal the waters of 'Hampstede Hethe' by building an embankment beneath the summit. The plan was a failure and it was not until 1693 that William Paterson, an enterprising Scot who had helped to found the Bank of England, had another try. He did this with partners known as the 'Society of Hampstead Aqueducts', but more generally as the Hampstead Waterworks Company.

What they did was to use the various tributaries of the River Fleet, one arm of which began near the Vale of Health and the other at Kenwood. The Highgate side was in operation by 1698 and it is still not clear when the Hampstead water was first utilised. In harnessing the waters of the Fleet the Company constructed the Highgate and Hampstead Ponds, which acted as reservoirs.

The undertaking was absorbed into the New River Company in 1859 and again later into the predecessors of the Thames Water Authority. The holders of the shares of the old Society of Hampstead Aqueducts still receive a perpetual annual sum of £3500 although no water is used. In fact, the water was never particularly drinkable and was last used, mainly for industrial purposes, in 1936.

*142. Highgate Ponds.* By T. Hastings, c1825. This is, presumably, the present boating pond by Millfield Lane, but none of the buildings shown matches any for which we have clear illustrations. It could be that the multi-sided building by the side of the pond is related to the workings of the Hampstead Water Company.

*143. North Road.* The shops shown on this postcard of *c*1906 have since been swept away by the building of houses along this stretch. The old Castle Inn and Castle Yard are towards the left. The butcher's run by Lake on the right was taken in 1920 by W.R. Mudd, who later transferred his business to the High Street.

# The Traders

For much of the 19th century there were as many shops in North Road and Hill as in the High Street, though most of the important ones were in the main street. This proliferation disappeared as Highgate School expanded and as it became possible to travel easily to places like Holloway Road, where stores like Jones Bros., with large departments selling such items as haberdashery and hats, effectively, if gradually, put small shops out of business. Significant changes have taken place in more recent years as shop rents, in line with house prices, have risen to the point where it would be difficult to sell household goods with much profit. Their places have been taken by offices masquerading as shops selling houses. However, Highgate must be grateful that the site areas in the High Street are generally too small to attract the multiple names and there is still *some* individuality to its shops.

The more leisurely, cheap-labour days of retailing have gone, so that no more may a shopper sit calmly in her vehicle outside as the shop assistant comes out to serve. Gone, too, are the many delivery vans and bicycles that dealt directly with the houses.

There are, though, still some reminders of former times. For example, two shops in the High Street have built-out canopies which signify their previous existence as butchers – the canopies kept the sun off the meat. The patisserie at no. 4 South Grove carries on a bakery use which may be traced back to 1745. Bailey and Saunders, pharmacists at no. 64 High Street, are in premises which were at one time the White Lion pub, and after that were taken by Thomas Dunn, who manufactured soda water here for medicinal purposes – one of his large vats has recently been unearthed. The prescription books for this business date back to 1813, and they include such customers' names as Lord Mansfield and Michael Faraday, who stayed occasionally in Hornsey Lane, Thomas Coutts and the Duke of St Albans.

The weather-boarded premises at no. 58 High Street are a reminder of Marriott, the corndealer. Kent's Yard, by its side (and now enclosed by gates), was named from George Kent, cornchandler, a previous occupant. The Corner Shop, what used to be Walton, Hassell and Port at the junction with Southwood Lane, is undoubtedly the oldest grocery in the village. In 1799 James Poulter, grocer, was trading on this site. Opposite him, but now gone, was Attkins the pork butchers, one of the more notable sights of

144. *Attkins' butcher's shop.* Elizabeth Attkins was running this celebrated pork butchers at no. 55 High Street at the time of this photograph. The premises were rebuilt in 1893. The Prince of Wales pub, to the left, is one of Highgate's newer drinking places: it began in 1864 as a beer shop.

145. *Newsagent and Tobacconist of Elizabeth Perkins at 34 Highgate Hill in 1923.* This photograph reproduced by kind permission of Alan Sanders, is a reminder of broadsheet newspapers and smoking brands of the past.

the village for the stout-hearted, for as late as the early part of this century pigs, with their throats cut, were kept in tubs of brine behind the shop; a horse used to work a large fly wheel which minced meat for sausages. The family's name may still be seen on the brickwork of the building.

Nor should we forget the oldest of the estate agents, Prickett and Ellis, whose principal work in early days was surveying, valuation, rent collection and general carpentry. The firm was founded by John Prickett in 1767; one of his descendants, Frederick, born in 1821, was, at the age of 21, the first historian of Highgate. From the end of the 19th century the business has been managed by the Ellis family, and some indication of the growth of property prices since then is the fact that in 1925 the total turnover was about £250,000. Sturt and Tivendale are comparative newcomers, having been in the village only 70 years!

Other long established businesses include Fisher and Sperr, surely one of the best-stocked second-hand booksellers in the country, which has been run by the redoubtable John Sperr for over 40 years. The Howe family recently sold their busy newsagent's shop in the High Street which they had run since 1920, and Barclays Bank occupy the building of the London and South Western Bank, which they absorbed, specially built in 1895 for banking purposes. Wylie's bakery opened a branch in Highgate in 1923 and it has been in its present premises since 1935.

The most picturesque of the traders were the blacksmiths. Several existed in the more spacious premises in North Road, but the one most commonly illustrated is Dodd's forge, situated where the buses now turn round at the top of the hill. It was a ramshackle place, with a tree growing through its roof, and a smithy may be traced back to this site in 1664; it was demolished in 1896.

*146. Highgate High Street, c1890.* The premises shown stretch from no. 62, which was then Garrett's the butchers, down to the corner with Townsend's Yard. At that time no. 48 was a pub called The Cooper's Arms.

OLD HOUSES,
HIGH STREET, HIGHGATE.

147. *William Lowe, boot and shoemaker, no. 80 Southwood Lane.* Photograph, 1911. The plaque to the left advertises A. Rowles of Fortis Green, chimney sweep and carpet beater.

## TRADERS OF ANOTHER ERA

Below is a list of Highgate traders included in an 1805 Directory. Many of the occupations have long gone.

John Addison, ale brewer, High Street

Joseph Aldworth, plumber, glazier and painter, High Street

George Astill, carpenter, joiner and undertaker, High Street

Samuel Attkins, butcher, High Street

Edward Austin, farmer, Irongate House, North Road

John Bachelour, carpenter, Hornsey Lane

Bellamy, The Bull

Joseph Blackley, The Rose and Crown

Boston, locksmith and bellhanger, High Street

James Bristow, The Angel

James Buckland, ale brewer, High Street

Elizabeth Cleaves, tobacco pipe manufacturer, Hornsey Lane

William Constable, hatter, High Street

Rev Dr A. Crombie, Holly House Academy, Kentish Town Hill

Thomas Davies, pastrycook, Highgate House, Hornsey Hill

Richard Dermot, perfumer, High Street

Joseph Drake, shopkeeper, High Street

William Drummond, The Fox, Kentish Town Hill

John Dutton, The Wrestler

William Eaton, apothecary and chemist, High Street

William Englefield, Red Lion and Sun

Thomas Ensor, undertaker, High Street

William Farey, taylor, Hornsey Hill

William Fitch, baker, High Street

Gabell, surgeon, High Street

John George, farrier and smith, High Street

Elizabeth Graves, tin shop, Hornsey Hill

John Goodman, The Red Lion

James Gray, baker, opposite the Ponds

Martha Green, shopkeeper, High Street

James Groves, grocer and cheesemonger, High Street

Charles Harding, hairdresser, High Street

Joseph Haughton, shoemaker, High Street

Samuel Holmes, shoemaker, High Street

William Horrell, plumber, glazier and painter, North Road

James James, stonemason, High Street

John Jaques, farmer, High Street

William Johnson, circulating library and stationer, High Street

Kearton and Sheldon, Ladies' Boarding School, Hornsey Hill

William Kemp, whip, collar and harness manufacturer, High Street

William King, Academy, Hornsey Hill

William Lea, coachmaker and wheeler, High Street

Mary Like, dealer in earthenware, High Street

Chace Lyne, butcher, opposite the Ponds

Andrew Mackey, greengrocer, High Street

Isabella Marshall, mantua-maker, opposite the Ponds

Thomas Martinson, The Flask

Richard Mayell, cooper, High Street

Mary Melton and Son, bricklayers and plaisterers, Southwood Lane

James Menton, butcher, Hornsey Hill

Benjamin Mitchell, Coach and Horses

John Newson, apothecary, Highgate

David Nicholls, coach and cart wheeler, High Street

William Norman, linen draper and haberdasher, High Street

William Ogle, shopkeeper, High Street

John Osborn, shopkeeper and potato warehouse, High Street

William Osborn, Bull and Wrestlers

Miss Owens, Boarding School, Hornsey Hill

Thompson Pater, surgeon and man midwife, near the Ponds

George Peach, Castle Inn

Mrs Philips, Boarding School, Grove

J. Pickford, sea coal warehouse, High Street

Joseph Pitkin, taylor, High Street

Thomas Pooley, baker, High Street

James Poulter, tea dealer and grocer, High Street

Powis, Infirmary for Horses, North Road

Ann Prickett, carpenter, joiner and undertaker High Street

Recknell, cooper, High Street

Benjamin Richards, Gate House and Assembly

Z. Rose, shopkeeper, High Street

Richard Sadleir, appraiser and auctioneer, High Street

James Salisbury, stone mason, High Street

John Schneider, nurseryman and seedsman, Kentish Town hill

Charles Scudamore, surgeon, Highgate

Miss Smith, Boarding School, High Street

David Southo, Green Dragon

Mrs Margaret Stevenson, haberdasher and milliner, High Street

Samuel Stevenson, linen draper, High Street

George Stringer, farmer and cowkeeper, opposite the Ponds

Elizabeth Sutton, fruiterer, Hornsey hill

Thomas Taunton, optician, North Road

Miss Ann Teulon, Boarding School, Hornsey Lane

Thornburgh, fisherman, High Street

James Townshend, bricklayer and plaisterer, High Street

John Upton, farmer, High Street

Richard Watkin, farmer, near the Ponds

Robert Ward, gardener, Southwood Lane

Richard Wells, The Old Crown

William Wetherell, surgeon, near the Grove
John Williams, coal merchant and chandler, High Street
Henry Williams, gardener, Southwood Lane
Susannah Worley, plumber, glazier and painter, Southwood Lane

Robert Wyke, jeweller, North Road
S. Yexley, The Cooper's Arms
Thomas Yorke, locksmith and bellhanger, High Street

*148. Hayhoe's forge, no. 45 North Road.*
This photograph of the 1880s proclaims that the forge was founded in 1760. By 1932 it was a petrol station.

The Old Forge,          High Street,          Highgate

London & South Western Bank · Highgate ·
Truefill & Watson · Architects ·
5. Bloomsbury Sq. W.C.

The Highgate Pharmacy in 1829

## GARDENS FOR ENTERTAINING

The views of the grounds of Southwood and of Mr Bodkin's house (*Illustrations 51* and *103*) give some idea of the delightful and extensive gardens in which the wealthier disported themselves. The largest grounds were those of Holly Lodge, where the Baroness Burdett-Coutts made ample use of them for charitable as well as private purposes. The *Highgate Parish Magazine* in 1871 reported that in the past year she had entertained 'the laundresses from the Temple, our own almswomen and occupants of parish houses, 1140 boys from the schools of Westminster and Highgate, thirty haymakers, the Empress of Brazil, the Emperor Napoleon and the Archbishop of Canterbury.'

Sometimes gardens would be opened for charitable purposes, such as those of Caen Wood Towers in Hampstead Lane. In more recent years those of Beechwood nearby (until they were withdrawn from public view and curiosity) were frequently opened to a public happy to pay an entrance fee to a charity to enjoy them.

Offensive security now also reigns at Witanhurst. Here were once the famous tennis parties organised by Sir Arthur and Lady Crosfield. As the caption to *The Tatler* report (*Illustration 153*) says, these were held immediately after the Wimbledon tournament, in aid of some charity chosen by the Crosfields.

149. (*Facing top*) *The Old Forge, Highgate High Street.* Dodd's famous smithy, with a tree growing through its roof, stood on the site of the bus terminus. It was demolished in 1895.

150. (*Facing left*) *The London and South Western Bank.* The same year as Dodd's smithy was demolished there was building work on the other side of the road, where this bank building was being erected. It is now Barclays Bank.

151. (*Facing right*) *The Highgate Pharmacy in 1829.* A sketch made in 1962 from an unknown source. At the date mentioned Thomas Dunn was at no. 44 High Street, next to Townsend's Yard. He did not move to his better known premises at no. 64, today occupied by Bailey and Saunders, until 1832.

# Society at Play

*Sir Arthur & Lady Crosfield*

152. *Sir Arthur and Lady Crosfield.*

## SIR ARTHUR AND LADY CROSFIELD'S TENNIS PARTY.

MR. CAZALET AND LADY LINLITHGOW

COLONEL MAYES, LADY MARY ASHLEY-COOPER, THE COUNTESS OF MAR AND KELLIE, AND MR. MISHU

PRINCESS OBOLENSKI

COUNTESS RABEN AND MR. F. R. SCOVEL

LADY WARD

Sir Arthur and Lady Crosfield's annual tennis party at their house at West Hill, Highgate, which they give in aid of the North Islington Infant Welfare Fund, was as big a success as ever. It is always held immediately after Wimbledon, and most of the stars" appear. There is also usually an American tournament in which everyone plays. The Marchioness of Linlithgow, who is with Mr. Cazalet, is a daughter of Sir Frederick Milner, Bart. Colonel Mayes is about the best-known man in the lawn tennis world of England; Lady Mary Ashley-Cooper is Lord and Lady Shaftesbury's daughter, and Lady Mar and Kellie is Lord Shaftesbury's sister

153. *(Above) Tennis Party at Witanhurst.* From *The Tatler*, 21 July, 1926.

154. (Above right) An interior photograph of Witanhurst, a house said to be, after Buckingham Palace, the largest private residence in London.

155. *(Below right) Lord and Lady Southwood in the garden of their house, Southwood Court.* The photograph was taken in the 1930s at one of the many charity garden parties held in the grounds of their house.

156. *(Facing Page) Advertisement for a Colonial Garden Party at Caen Wood Towers.* This event, in 1886, was held in aid of the Finsbury Park Young Men's Christian Association. At the time the house was owned by Francis Reckitt, the dye manufacturer.

A

# COLONIAL GARDEN PARTY

— AND —

## STRAWBERRY & CREAM FESTIVAL,

*Will be held by the kind permission of* FRANCIS RECKITT, Esq., *in the Beautiful and Spacious Grounds (some 13 acres in extent), of*

## CAEN-WOOD TOWERS, HAMPSTEAD LANE, HIGHGATE,

On Wednesday Afternoon & Evening, JUNE 30th, 1886.——

Under the direction of the Ladies' Council and General Committee of the

## Finsbury Park Hall Young Men's Christian Association.

---

### THE GROUNDS WILL BE OPENED AT TWO O'CLOCK.

---

The following additional attractions will be added to that of the Grounds:—

LAWN TENNIS (2 or 3 Courts).     ARCHERY GROUND.

A POPULAR BRASS BAND will play a selection of Music from 2.30 to 7.30.

A GYMNASTIC DISPLAY by Members of the FINSBURY PARK HALL GYMNASIUM, under the direction of GEO. L. MÉLIO.

BOY HAND-BELL RINGERS from "DR. BARNARDO'S HOME."

OPEN AIR CONCERT.

SELECTION OF INSTRUMENTAL MUSIC, by "THE NORTH LONDON VIOLIN CLASS."

---

It is simply impossible to describe the beauty of CAEN-WOOD TOWERS. Within the Grounds will be found a MINIATURE LAKE, LOVELY WALKS AND BOWERS, GROVES, GROTTOES, COOL RETREATS, together with a bountiful supply of STRAWBERRIES AND CREAM, LIGHT REFRESHMENTS, &c., (for which a slight charge will be made); and at

## 5-30—TEA will be served in a Grand Marquee,

PRESIDED OVER BY

## Sir CHARLES TUPPER, G.C.M.G., C.B., High Commissioner for Canada, &c.

SUPPORTED BY

HUGH MATHESON, Esq.              W. HIND SMITH, Esq.

E. J. KENNEDY, Esq.     R. C. MORGAN, Esq.     J. L. AUKLAND, Esq.     Mrs. AUKLAND.

And other Ladies and Gentlemen.

---

## SINGLE TICKETS *(including Tea)*, 2/6;   FAMILY TICKETS *(admitting Four)*, 7/6.

A limited number only of Tickets will be issued (until 24th June), so that an early application should be made to

JOHN ORCHARD, General Secretary, Y.M.C.A.,

255, Seven Sisters Road, N.

*Cheques and Postal Orders preferred in payment.*

CAEN-WOOD TOWERS can be reached by Tram to the top of Highgate Hill (five minutes' walk), or by Rail to Highgate station, G.N.R. (15 minutes' walk). Should the weather prove unfavourable on the Wednesday, permission has been given for the following day.

ST. PANCRAS ... COLLECTION.

# Famous Names

The list of notable people who have lived in Highgate is long. Some have been transitory and others, like Coleridge, were very much part of village life. The poet lived at no. 3 The Grove, the same house that J.B. Priestley, the writer, occupied for six years from 1933, at the height of his popularity. Next door, at no. 2, the musician, Yehudi Menuhin, lived from 1959 to 1983, during that time lending his name and energy to a number of Highgate causes. Other famous names in The Grove were Christopher Hassall, the librettist and playwright at no. 8, and Roger Fry, the artist who also popularised the paintings of Cèzanne in this country, was born at no. 6 – his father was Sir Edward Fry, Lord Chief Justice. Other residents included Robert Donat the actor (no. 8), John Drinkwater the poet and playwright (no. 9) and the actress Gladys Cooper (nos. 1–2).

A remarkable woman lived at no. 22 Southwood Lane from 1863–79. Mary Kingsley, daughter of an anthropologist and niece of the writer Charles Kingsley, remained at home until she was 31, but her father's death encouraged her to travel to the Congo to continue his research. Travelling in the most inhospitable terrain she dressed in a black skirt, high-necked blouse and a hat, and she armed herself with an umbrella. It was, in fact, the voluminous folds of the skirt that saved her life when she fell into an animal trap lined with spikes. Intrepid to the last she returned to previously unexplored territory and again in 1900, to nurse Boer prisoners in South Africa, where she died of enteric fever.

The redoubtable Florence Nightingale stayed at no. 37 Highgate West Hill in 1859 to recuperate after the Crimean War, while the house was owned by Mary and William Howitt. The latter were in a good position, halfway up the hill, to complain in print at the cruelty suffered by horses as they struggled to the summit.

Further down the hill, in 1907, John Betjeman, then aged one, arrived with his family at no. 31. He was later a pupil at Highgate School where he was taught occasionally by T.S. Eliot. One of his best known poems,*Summoned by Bells*, portrayed delightfully and with much perception the tram ride up from Kentish Town and the surroundings of Highgate West Hill.

On North Hill lived Charles Green, a notable balloonist, at the aptly named Aerial Cottage, no. 33 North Hill. He began life as a fruiterer in his father's business but took an early interest in the means of flight pioneered by Montgolfier. He made his first ascent from Green Park in 1821 in a balloon filled

157. *Mary Kingsley (1862–1900).*

158. *Michael Faraday (1791–1867).* Faraday is said to have sometimes stayed in the Hornsey Lane area; his name is recorded in the records of the Highgate Pharmacy as a customer.

*159. Four men in a basket* – Charles Green and friends.

*160. Mary Howitt.*

with hydrogen. After that he made a remarkable 526 ascents, even, in 1828, mounted on his pony. A tragedy was associated with his adventures when, in 1837, a fellow balloonist dropped from the basket using an experimental parachute which did not function. Despite such a dangerous life, Green died in his bed in Tufnell Park, aged 85.

A number of architects made Highgate their home. Sir James Pennethorne lived at Elm Court, a house (now demolished) between Lauderdale House and Fairseat, from 1842–64. He had been principal assistant to John Nash, to whom he was related, and although he was architect of a number of prestigious buildings, such as the Public Record Office, his main contribution to London topography is that he was in charge of creating such new roads as New Oxford Street, Endell Street and Commercial Street. Lewis Vulliamy, the designer of St Michael's church, lived at Cholmeley Lodge, and George Basevi the architect of Belgrave Square and other splendid buildings before his untimely death, was at The Elms in Fitzroy Park. Berthold Lubetkin, the designer of Highpoint, lived for two years in his own block, a rarity for an architect, as did the splendidly named Erno Goldfinger. Sir Thomas Bennett died in 1980, having lived at no. 19 North Road since 1932. His early architectural work had a lightness of touch – the Savile Theatre in Shaftesbury Avenue and John Barnes in Finchley Road are good examples, but it is unlikely that the more recent Royal Lancaster Hotel, or, indeed, the Hillcrest flats in Highgate, have many admirers.

A controversial resident of Pond House in Millfield Lane, was the Baroness Edith Summerskill. She was a feminist from her girlhood and was combative in that cause all her life. She was a fiery political speaker, popular in the Labour Party, but she never did achieve particularly high office. When she went to the Lords she concentrated on causes which she had had all her life – women's rights, abortion law reform, medical reform and the abolition of boxing.

The creative artists may well be the names which are plucked out to illustrate the attraction of Highgate, but in fact the character of the village has always been fairly conventional with its larger

*161. Charles Knight (1791–1873).* Knight was a prolific publisher of cheap educational aids to the newly literate classes. He lived at no. 128 Highgate Hill from 1835.

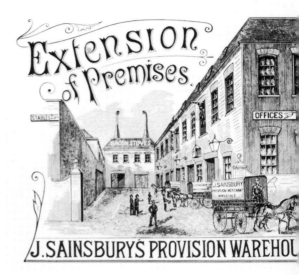

*162. Sainsbury's premises off Queen's Crescent, Kentish Town.*

*163. A.E. Housman (1859–1936).* The poet lodged at no. 17 North Road 1886–1905, and here wrote his famous poem *A Shropshire Lad*. (Courtesy of The National Portrait Gallery)

houses occupied by business or professional men. Two highly successful business men settled in Highgate, one a printer, the other a grocer.

The printer was Julius Elias, (Lord Southwood) whose name, now, means nothing to the general public. As a boy he was an office lad in the run-down factory of the Odhams brothers in Floral Street, Covent Garden. When the company was on the point of closure Elias offered to be salesman and by intuition, talent and hard work transformed the firm into the largest printing concern in the country. At its peak Odhams had several factories in Long Acre and a large plant at Watford. He published *John Bull*, a jingoistic but successful weekly. He invented magazines such as *Woman*, *Illustrated*, and *Picturegoer* and he eventually took a majority shareholding in the TUC's *Daily Herald*, building it up to be the largest selling daily newspaper. Its unlikely successor, *The Sun*, still has that claim.

Elias was a very wealthy man by the 1920s. He bought Southwood Court, off Southwood Lane, and later took over another large house, confusingly called Southwood, only to demolish it to add the grounds to his own.

Another rags-to-riches resident was John James Sainsbury. He was the son of a frame maker and had

164. *Dr Thomas Southwood Smith (1790–1861).* Smith was an energetic public health reformer, who stayed regularly with relatives at a house called Hillside in Fitzroy Park.

166. *Francis Bacon (1561–1626).* Scientist, politician and philosopher, who died at Arundel House in South Grove.

165. *Florence Nightingale (1820–1910).*

had a lot of experience living near street markets such as The Cut in Lambeth and Berwick Street. He opened his first grocers at 173 Drury Lane in 1869, when he was 25, in the same year as he married a dairyman's daughter. Their modest ambition was to have enough branches for each of their sons to manage, but even though his wife bore him six sons and five daughters (while still working actively in the business), they still had far more branches than sons by the time they got to their managerial age. The first branch was in Queen's Crescent, Kentish Town, and the Sainsburys moved into the house above it. The most important development was a branch opened in Croydon where, for the first time, they designed a shop that not only looked clean, a rare thing in food retailing, but was, which was even rarer. It was handsomely decorated with wood, marble and tiles and this set the style for Sainsbury's for a very long time. The rest is familiar history, and by the time that Sainsbury settled in Highgate in 1899, at no. 14 Broadlands Road, he was a very rich man.

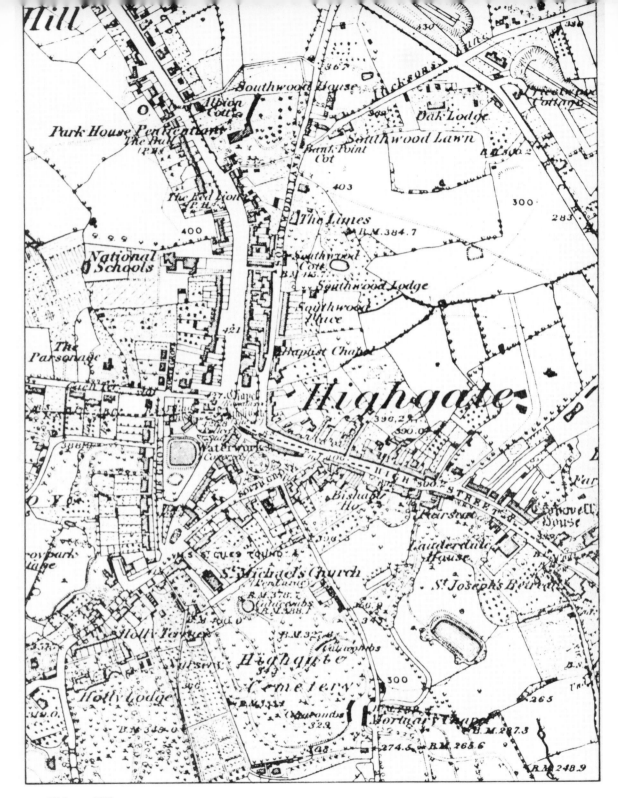

167. *Highgate, 1873.*

# A Built-up Area

Until about the 1880s Highgate virtually stopped in Southwood Lane. Fields then stretched to Muswell Hill, Crouch End and Finchley, themselves largely rural. Then the Ecclesiastical Commissioners gradually sold off parts of the old Bishop of London's estate and the roads on either side of North Hill were built. Hornsey Lane was developed, mainly by the Imperial Property Company, with very large houses for the *nouveau-riche*. The Miltons, the name for a group of streets on the other side of the Archway Road, were the result of the opening of Highgate Railway Station and were built for lower middle-class people – the burgeoning clerical class. Some reminders of the detached, better-class houses on Archway Road survive from the time that road was

pleasant to live by. Other streets were formed in the large gardens of the Southwood Lane mansions. Winchester Hall, on Highgate Hill, was demolished and its land developed. Further south the oddly-named Highgate New Town was completed, a mean array, with few exceptions, of unsanitary streets that was a development *towards* Highgate, rather than from it.

By the 1920s Highgate was almost complete, other than the Holly Lodge Estate. By and large it escaped the 1930s fashion for blocks of flats. The Cholmeley Park blocks replaced the old Cholmeley Lodge and, despite much protest, South Grove House was demolished for apartments. The most unusual blocks were those called Highpoint in North Hill, described by Le Corbusier as the 'seed of the vertical garden city'. They were designed by Lubetkin and initially some flats were let to low-income tenants, an experiment that was not a success.

*168. Wynnstay, Hornsey Lane.* This postcard shows one of the typical mansions erected on the newly fashionable Hornsey Lane from the 1870s.

169. *North Hill*. Postcard c1910.

170. *Jackson's Lane*. Postcard c1910.

*171. No. 42 Highgate High Street.* This house was owned in the early 19th century by the Townshend family, whose abbreviated name gave the yard next door its present title. The Townshends were builders who helped in the demolition of Ashurst House in South Grove. The coat-of-arms from that building was placed above the doorway of the Townshend house in the High Street – it can still be seen today. The Broadbent stationer's shop next door was gone by 1888.

*172. Highgate High Street, c1906.* The peacefulness of the High Street at the beginning of the age of the motor car may be seen here. On the right are the houses leading to the corner with Bisham Gardens. Judging from the tramway tracks this photograph was taken in the early part of the century before the tramway was electrified.

*173. Shepherd's Hill.* Postcard, 1911.

*174. The new Archway, Archway Road.* The new bridge, opened in August 1900, allowed a greater width of road and, most importantly, electrified trams to pass beneath it. It was designed by Alexander Binnie.

175. *Hampstead Lane*. Postcard, *c*1906.

176. *Southwood Lane*. Postcard, *c*1906.

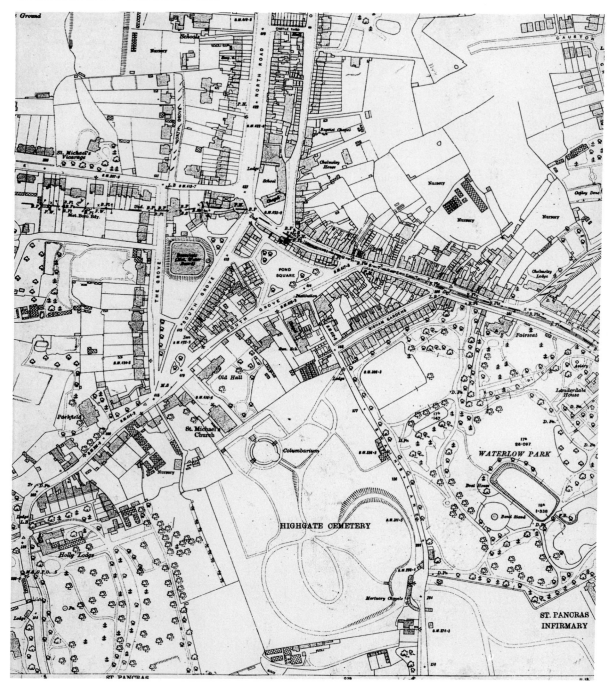

*177. Ordnance Survey of the Highgate area, 1914.*

# Index

Illustrations are indicated in bold type